Drone Footage
by Trey Smith
Branson, MO

All Glory to

He   Vav   He   Yod
5   6   5   10

Above is the name of God (YHVH) written in PreCannanite Hebrew.

Let me boldly state, it is the original PreFlood language of Earth. Or, perhaps better stated, "The Tongue of Angels & Men"

NASA FOOTAGE
EARTH FROM
SPACE

IN THE BEGINNING...

∞

According to our ancient texts, particularly the oldest, we are in a place that should not exist – a place that is a product of a larger place: Eternity and God Himself.

The book of Genesis is telling you that you are living in a tiny subset of a much LARGER and FAR MORE COMPLEX REALITY, that is teeming with life.

Beginning with Einstein and physics, we understand the material world to be nothing more than a clever illusion of "vibrations." And, according to the very same physics, when one looks deeply enough into the smallest particles of matter itself, infinity is in each one – the point of paradox. As if every particle of this place, this universe, this little world, is merely a pixel on a screen we can not see the other side of.

More than all this, none of it is random.

Going one step further, nearly all ancient texts, particularly the oldest, believe that eternity, "the place from which this place comes from," is God Himself
-- The Intelligent Source from which all creation extends to exist, Father of everything.

Thus, in science, it is with humble awe we find that the paradox is much greater than just eternity and the particle-pixels of Reality...

The paradox is everything.

GOD SAID THAT KNOWLEDGE WOULD INCREASE
FOR THOSE LIVING IN THE END.....

TREY'S NOTES

This Book is Special in History

This Book is Dedicated to YOU.

Shall we begin.....

Name of God YHVH beneath Means

Behold NAil Behold Hand

The GOD Truth

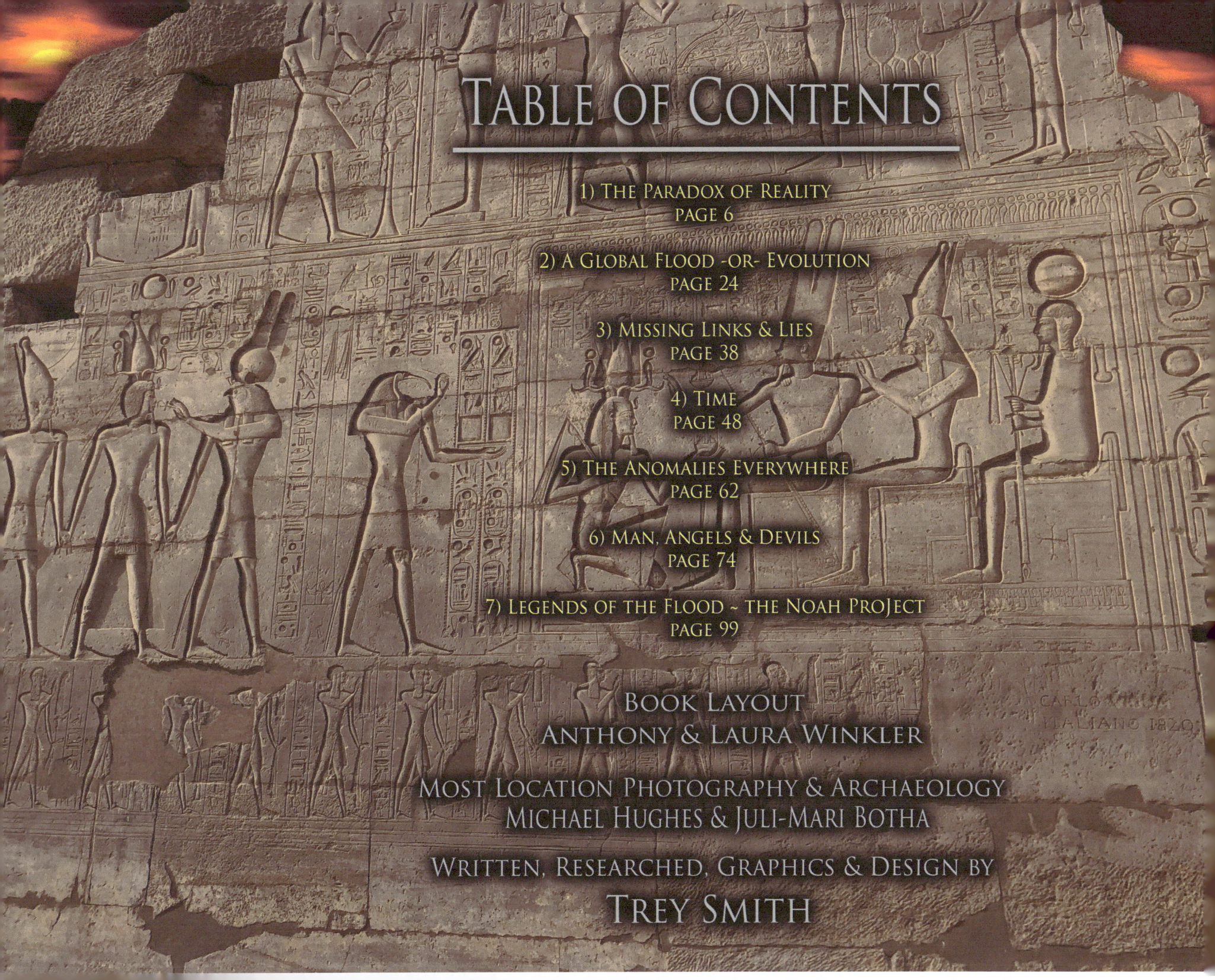

TABLE OF CONTENTS

1) THE PARADOX OF REALITY
PAGE 6

2) A GLOBAL FLOOD -OR- EVOLUTION
PAGE 24

3) MISSING LINKS & LIES
PAGE 38

4) TIME
PAGE 48

5) THE ANOMALIES EVERYWHERE
PAGE 62

6) MAN, ANGELS & DEVILS
PAGE 74

7) LEGENDS OF THE FLOOD ~ THE NOAH PROJECT
PAGE 99

BOOK LAYOUT
ANTHONY & LAURA WINKLER

MOST LOCATION PHOTOGRAPHY & ARCHAEOLOGY
MICHAEL HUGHES & JULI-MARI BOTHA

WRITTEN, RESEARCHED, GRAPHICS & DESIGN BY
TREY SMITH

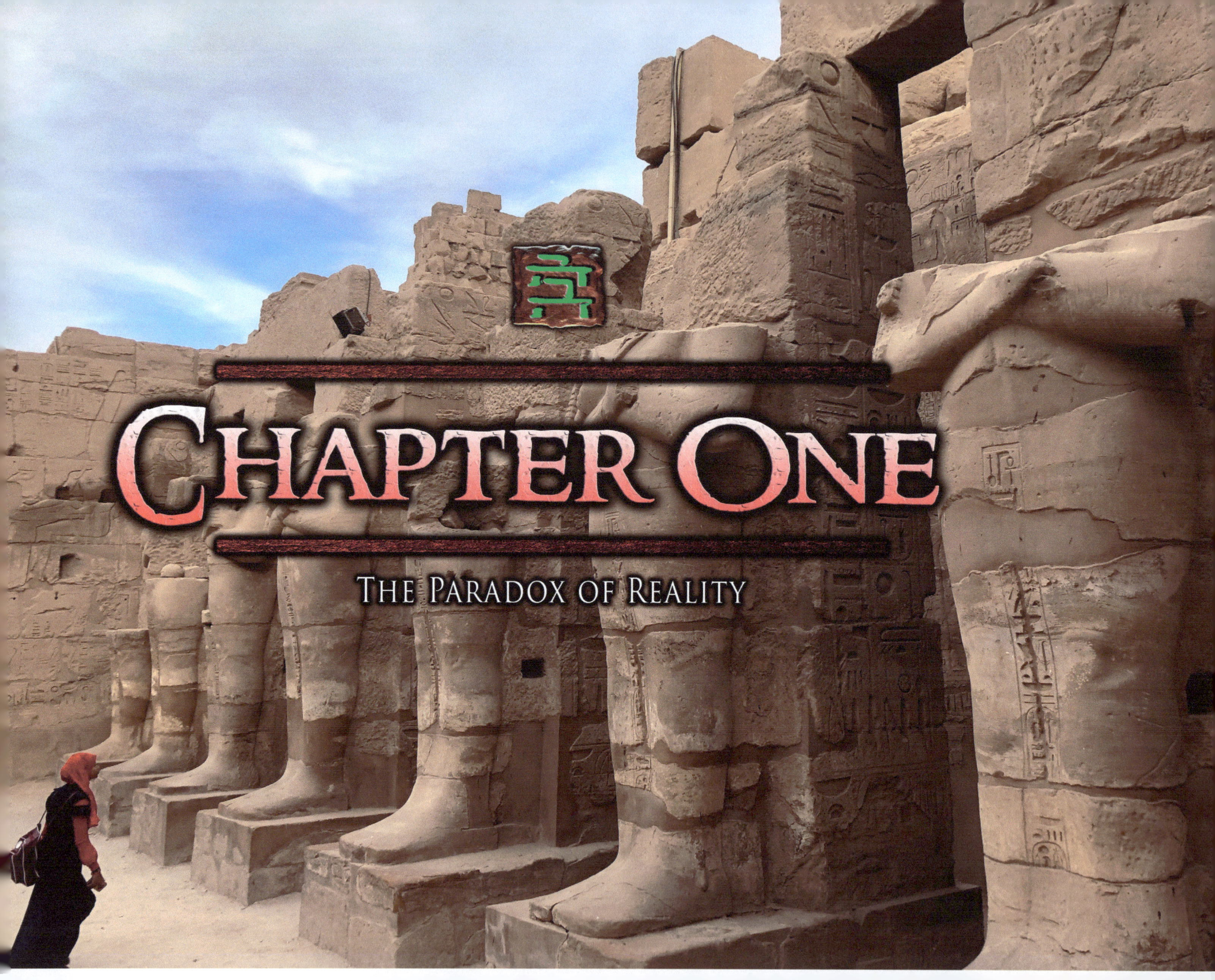

Chapter One

The Paradox of Reality

A SPECIAL OF PRAYER OF BLESSING IS ON EVERY READER OF THESE PAGES.

LET US START WITH AN INTRODUCTION TO WHY THE MATHEMATICS, SCIENCE & ANCIENT TEXTS OF THIS PLACE FIT TOGETHER LIKE A SPECIAL PUZZLE.

OUR GUIDE WILL BE THE CAMEL NAMED: MOSES.

22

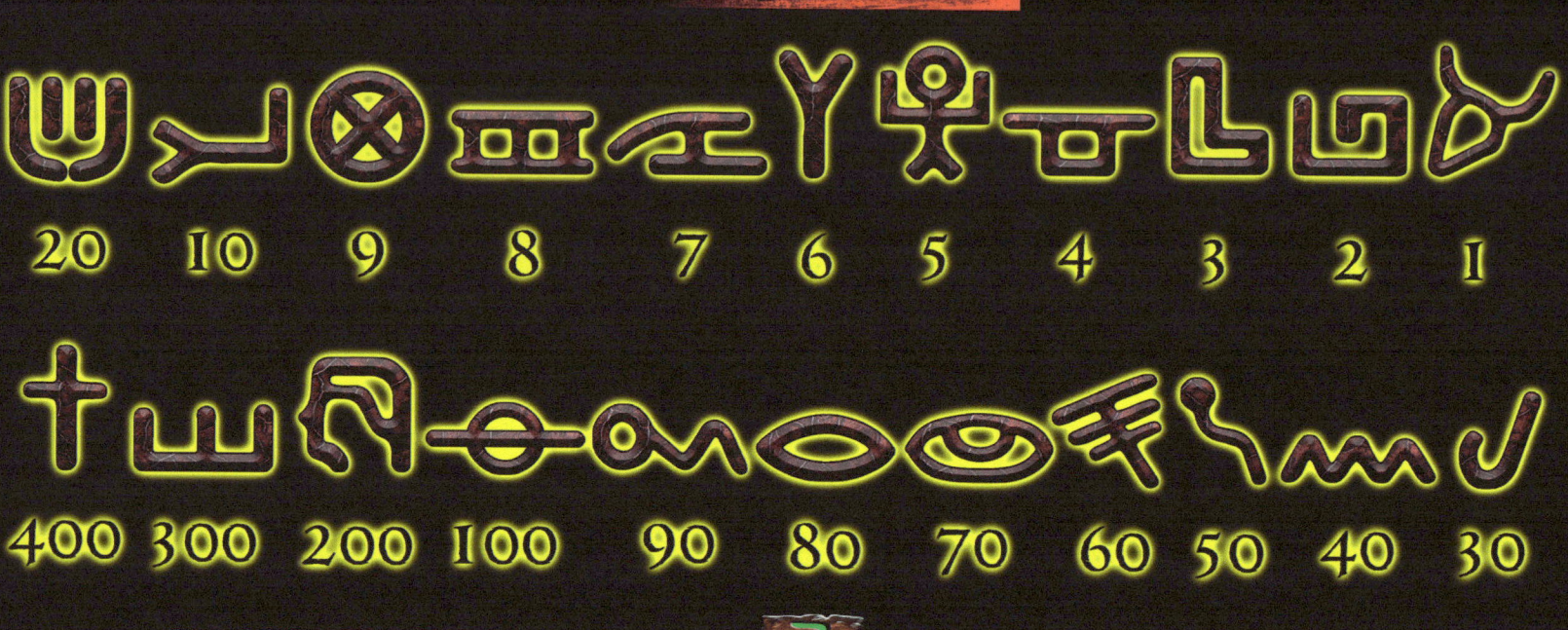

Above is Ancient Hebrew; sometimes called "PreCannanite."
The Alef is now a Bull's head with horns. Horns represent Authority.
All Languages Point towards Israel. Hebrews is both phonetic (like English) and Pictographic (like Ancient Egyptian). It is the Language from which you get every other later Language (like Egyptian and English).
Its first Two Letters are the "Alef" and the "Beit". Which is where you get the English word "Alphabet."
It has 22 Letters. Or, 11:11.
The Last Letter is the Tav. The Tav is the Cross.

22

אבגדהוזחטי
20 10 9 8 7 6 5 4 3 2 1

לםנמפעזקרשת
400 300 200 100 90 80 70 60 50 40 30

Above is Modern Hebrew.
The language reads from right to left. It begins with the Alef א which is the silent letter that starts everything, representing God.
The Alef is the first or Number One. It is comprised of two Yods י.
Each Yod equals Ten. Just as there are 10 Commandments, or 10 Plagues of Egypt, etc...
The Yod dangles like a spirit between Heaven and Earth. It is also called the Creation Point.
Between the two Yods is a Vav ו. The number six. The symbol for a man.

SEA OF GALILEE IN IMAGE

TREY SMITH
GOD IN A NUTSHELL

ALL GLORY & CREDIT TO

—— TRUTH IS IN THE JOURNEY ——

Beit 2

Beit is Symbol for Home.

To the Left is Actual PreCannanite Hebrew writing found in the Center of Hezekiah's Tunnel in Jerusalem, Israel.

Image from Trey Smith's God Dimension

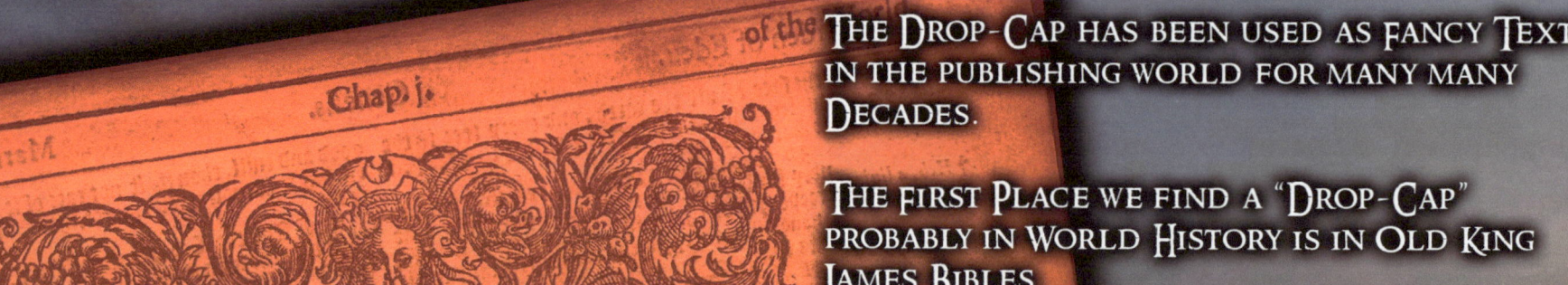

The Drop-Cap has been used as fancy Text in the publishing world for many many Decades.

The first Place we find a "Drop-Cap" probably in World History is in Old King James Bibles.

They were copying that "Drop-Cap effect" from the way it was in the Torah. And, accordingly, the Scribes were copying that from the way they Believed Moses got it exactly as it was written by God on top of Mount Sinai.

The Rabbis believe that the first Letter in the Torah that starts a sentence, a paragraph or a page, should give some Idea of what the entire Text will be about.

In the case of Genesis, or the Book of "Genes~is," that first Letter is the

Beit , or, the Second Letter of the Hebrew Alphabet.

The "Beit" is the Symbol for Home.

So, Everything from Genesis to Revelation is about "Home."

The Words "In the Beginning" start with the Hebrew "Beit"

Three Words Start Everything

In the Beginning

The word "Genesis" ("Bereishit" in Hebrew), or "In the Beginning" in English, are actually this beneath set of six symbols; just as Man (Adam) was created in six days.

The first symbol being **HOME**

Caves of Qumran

These caves were the "Essenes". John the Baptist who baptized Jesus was an Essene. The Jordan where he baptized is only miles away. These were the caves of John's friends.

Actual Isaiah Scroll found in Qumran Caves

The Caves of Qumran were discovered in 1947. They contained Scrolls (and Scroll fragments) of nearly every Old Testament book.

These Scrolls date back more than 2,000 years. Or, more precisely, to just before the time of Jesus Christ.

The Scrolls stunned the world, as they proved the Biblical Texts (unlike any Texts on Earth) were nearly identical to their ancient form; word for word.

The Book of Enoch was also found in these caves.

MANETHO

The secular education world has chosen to use Manetho, a priest of both Thoth and Marduk, who lived at the time of the Greeks in the 3rd century BC, for their Egyptian history, upon which they have based world history.

You will often hear it said that Egyptian history is "rock-solid" in its time-lines. Nothing could further from reality.

The truth is: They have pulled what they like from Manetho's "Aegyptiaca" history, and ignored the rest. Manetho does however do us grand favors by matching the Egyptian gods with the Greek gods; like a Rosetta Stone of Demons & Devils. By "Golden Age of gods" (not to be confused with the "Golden Age of Prosper" for Egypt following Joseph) they are referring to a mixture of events slightly before and after the flood.

Additionally, you will notice that Manetho's history, clearly filtered through Nimrod & Sumeria, with a twist of knowledge from books like Enoch, is actually telling the Biblical story.

Manetho's Aegyptiaca (History of Egypt)

5. Mestraim (matches with Genesis 10) lived not long after the flood. For after the flood, Cham (or Ham), son of Noah, begat Aegyptus or Mestraim, who was the first to set out to establish himself in Egypt, at the time when the tribes began to disperse this way and that (following Babel). Now the whole time from Adam to the flood was 2242 years

12 The Zodiac has an equal number of parts, 360 (this comes from Enoch's Calendar). So, it came to pass that the reigns of the gods who ruled among them for six generations in six dynasties (structured in lots of sets of six just like the Sumerian King's list).

Manetho's "Golden Age of gods"

Sumerian King's List

1 Total, 969 years.
4. Cronos (Saturn/Enki), for 401 years.
5. Osiris and Isis, for 35 years.
6. Typhon, for 29 years.
Demigods:
7. Orus, for 20 years.
8. Ares, for 23 years.
9. Anubis, 17 years.
10. Hercules, for 15 years.
11. Apollo, for 25 years.
12. Ammon, for 30 years.
13. Tithoes, for 27 years
14. Sosus, for 32 years.
15. Zeus (represents Marduk, son of Enki, Jupiter), for 20 years.

Drone Footage by Trey Smith
Banias, Pan's Cave
Base of Mt. Hermon

.....And Enoch was NOT for God took him. ~ Gen 5:21-24

ENOCH

The Book of Enoch is a Controversial Text. It was excluded from the Modern Bible.

However, It is Qutoed from by Jude (the Half Brother of Jesus).

Additionally, It Prophecies repeatedly of the: "Coming of the Son of Man."

This is How Jesus Referred to Himself Many, Many Times.

The Book of Enoch does NOT read like a Pseudepigrapha (or Bogus) Text. It reads More Like a Treasure Chest of Prophetic Keywords that Can Light up Books like Revelation as would a Bulb in a Dark Room.

You have the Old Testament, the New Testament; and, Enoch would actually be the Prophetic Voice or Witness Crying out from Before the Flood.

Enoch was the Seventh (7th) from Adam. Or the Great Grandfather of Noah. His Document would Certainly have been on that Boat.

If we Count Enoch, then there are Three Major Apocalyptic Writings.

These would Be Revelation by John in the New Testament, the Book of Daniel from the Old Testament, And Thirdly, Enoch from the Pre-Flood World.

Pan's Cave
A Pagan Sacrifice Site At Base Mount Hermon

Neph Children

Peru

Image courtesy Brien Foerster

A Trey Smith / God in a Nutshell project

You have many Unexplained things on this planet, such as bodies that do not fit the "norm."

Your Bible and Enoch are describing a very strange PreFlood World ~ with "bleed-overs" into modern history.

These strange things are found at occult sites in Peru.

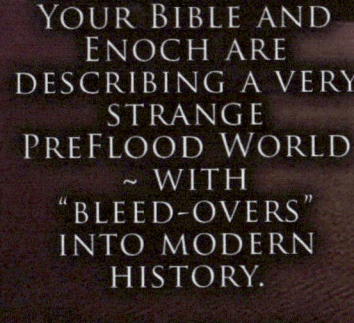

Images by Brien Foerster

Jude Quotes Enoch

"Even the Angels which kept not their first estate, but left their own habitation (Oiketerion), he hath reserved in everlasting chains under darkness unto the judgment of the great day." ~ Jude 1:6

Oiketerion

This word Oiketerion has a dual meaning. It is saying these beings traded their higher level "Heavenly Bodies" for three dimensional temporal bodies of flesh. The text says they bred strange children.

ENOCH
Scribe of Righteousness

Joseph's Grain Storage facility in Egypt seen in image

was brought in before this cast of Fallen Angels that had played "God" with mankind. The Fallen Angels, Demons & their offspring would later be worshipped as gods. They knew Enoch had a Relationship with the True God ~ Thus they feared him.

"And heal the earth which the angels have corrupted, and proclaim the healing of the earth, that they may heal .... And that all the children of men may not perish through all the secret things that the 8 Watchers have disclosed and have taught their sons." ~ Enoch 10

They asked him to make Prayers for their forgiveness. This was God's Response:

"You thought you had **SECRETS** yet all the Mysteries had not yet been revealed to you, Little did you know, You only knew the **WORTHLESS ONES.** You shall have No Peace for ALL Eternity." ~ Enoch 16

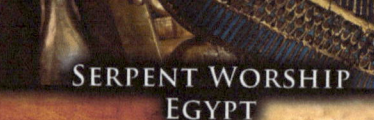

Serpent Worship Egypt

MOUNT HERMON

"By the order of the most high and holy god, those who swear an oath proceed from here."

The "god" is probably Baal-Hermon.

~Translation by Derek Gilbert

An Ancient Stela was Discovered atop Mt. Hermon
which honored the Fall of the Angels & Azazel.

Trey Smith sits on an Ancient Greek Pillar at the "Devil's Mouth" of Pan's Cave on the Base of Mount Hermon and reads from Enoch about the Fall of the Angels.

This was an Ancient Child Sacrifice Site for the Sumerians, the Babylonians, the Greeks, and the Romans.

It is also the Mount of Transfiguration where Jesus changed in form before the Disciples.

It was a Message to Darkness.

This is Also the Exact Spot where Jesus Pointed at Peter and said:

"Get Behind Me Satan!"

Greek God Pan

GENESIS 6

6 When man began to increase in number on the earth and daughters were born to them, 2 the sons of God (Bene-Ha Elohim ~ Angels, or in this context, Fallen Angels) saw that the daughters of men were beautiful, and they came down and took wives of any of them they chose.

3 Then the Lord said, "My Spirit will not contend with man forever, for they are mortal; their days will be a hundred and twenty years."

4 The Nephilim were on the earth in those days—and also afterward—when the sons of God went to the daughters of men and had children by them. They were the heroes (legends) of old, men of renown.

5 The Lord saw how great the wickedness of the man had become on the earth, and that every inclination of the thoughts of the human heart was only evil all the time. 6 It grieved the Lord that He had made Man, and his heart was deeply troubled. 7 So the Lord said, "I will wipe from the face of the earth the human race I have created.

8 But Noah found favor in the eyes of the Lord.

ENOCH 6

1. And it came to pass when the children of men had multiplied that in those days were born unto them beautiful and comely daughters. 2. And the angels, the children of the heaven, saw and lusted after them, and said to one another: 'Come, let us choose us wives from among the children of men and beget us children.'

3. And Semjâzâ, was their leader....

6. And they were in all two hundred; who descended in the days of Jared on the summit of Mount Hermon.

10

1. Then said the Most High, the Holy and Great One spake, and sent Uriel to the son of Lamech, and said to him: 2. 'Go to Noah and tell him in my name "Hide thyself!" and reveal to him the end that is approaching: that the whole earth will be destroyed, and a deluge is about to come upon the whole earth, and will destroy all that is on it. 3. And now instruct him that he may escape and his seed may be preserved for all the generations of the world.' 4. And again the Lord said to Raphael: 'Bind Azâzêl hand and foot, and cast him into the darkness.'

.....And Enoch was NOT for God took him. ~ Gen 5:21-24

6. And they were in all two hundred (Fallen Angels); who descended in the days of Jared on the summit of Mount Hermon, and they called it Mount Hermon, because they had sworn and bound themselves by mutual imprecations upon it.

Enoch 6:6

Enoch writes about the Pre-flood World and Fallen Angels as if it is common place to him. The same as you might write about Driving your car Today... But, to someone in the Ancient World you Driving your car might sound as Crazy magical Madness.

He Writes as One with Authority.

Semjâzâ and Azâzêl are the Two leaders of the Two Hundred Fallen Angels. Who "took Wives" of Mankind (this could imply by Force).

They Began Mixing Animals with Animals (Genes with Genes); Distorting Creation. They began teaching the Men the "Arts of War", and the Women to be Objects of Seduction.

They Taught the Summoning of Devils and Witchcraft for Guidance of Life.

They Taught the "Value of the Precious Stones" (Gold, Silver, etc...). They Birthed the Financial Systems that one's Worth is measured in the Illusions of Shiny Rocks... Skewing Everything. That men had Power over another by this means.

In Short, They came in to Play Little gods with mankind.

Their Children were Part Man / Part Angel ~ called the Nephilim. As is covered in,

Genesis 6

Trey Smith Pointing Towards Mt. Hermon from Replica of "Jesus Boat" on Sea of Galilee

Just as there were Two Trees in the Garden... A Choice... I think we are going to find that History also has these same Two paths...

A Choice...

And All of the seeming Variations and Possibilities are but an Illusion.

God Says: Choose this Day Whom you serve.

And, that Seemingly Mythological "Garden of Eden" may become Strangely Real in this Journey.

Genesis 3:1: "Now the serpent was more (Witchy) crafty (ā·RÛM) than any other beast of the field that the LORD God had made."

When they Ate of the Tree of Knowledge of Good and Evil.... The Word for "Naked" right Afterwards is: ā·RÛM

Just as Mankind has selected the worshippers of Devils for its History; when Adam and Eve ate of the Tree, they were ā·RÛM

They had taken on a Quality of the Serpent.

World History

Manetho

Your universities and scholars have largely based your ancient history timelines for world history on the writtings of Manetho.
As we will see later, Manetho believed in the Garden of Eden, and Adam and Eve... Your scholars failed to mention that did they? Manetho was a pagan priest of Thoth of Egypt. He also believed demons and fallen angels to be the "good guys."

The truth is all your ancient texts (particularly the oldest) are all telling the same account... a preflood world, a global flood, fallen angels, etc...

These cultures lived at the time of the things they are writting; making it especially hard to believe they are making it all up... and all "making up" the same story no-less.

Your "Modern Scholars" have simply taken what they have "liked" of recorded history, and ignored the rest.

When Alexander the Great conquered the world for the Greeks; he commissioned the cultures to give their history so the "Wisdom of the World" could be known and stored.

For the history of Egypt (upon which your current ancient history is based) that would be Manetho. For Israel, that would be the Septuagint.

Septuagint

This is the one your scholars and universities hate and go to any length to reject.

It is the basis of your Bible.

The word means 70 as 70 scribes or rabbis compiled it word by word.

It gives the most concise history on Earth.

Yet, it tells nearly the same account as the pagan Manetho.

However, unlike Manetho, it paints devils, Satan, and fallen angels as "bad guys."

Chapter Two

A Global Flood ~or~ Evolution?

Sea of Galilee

PRE-FLOOD

An Examination by Trey Smith

T-Rex by Larion Polacsek

The Names in Genesis Tell the Biblical Story

Adam	Man
Seth	Appointed
Enosh	Mortal
Kenan	Sorrow
Mahalalel	The Blessed God
Jared	Shall come down
Enoch	Teaching
Methuselah	His Death shall bring
Lamech	The Despairing
Noah	Rest & Comfort

If we take the Names in Genesis in the Blood-line going from Adam to Noah ~ the Literal Meaning of the Names Tells the Biblical Story. Notice there are exactly Ten (10) Generations from Adam to Noah. Ten is God's Number of Completion. It is also a Universal Whole Number

It would be difficult to believe a Set of Scribes concocted that in the Genesis Text.

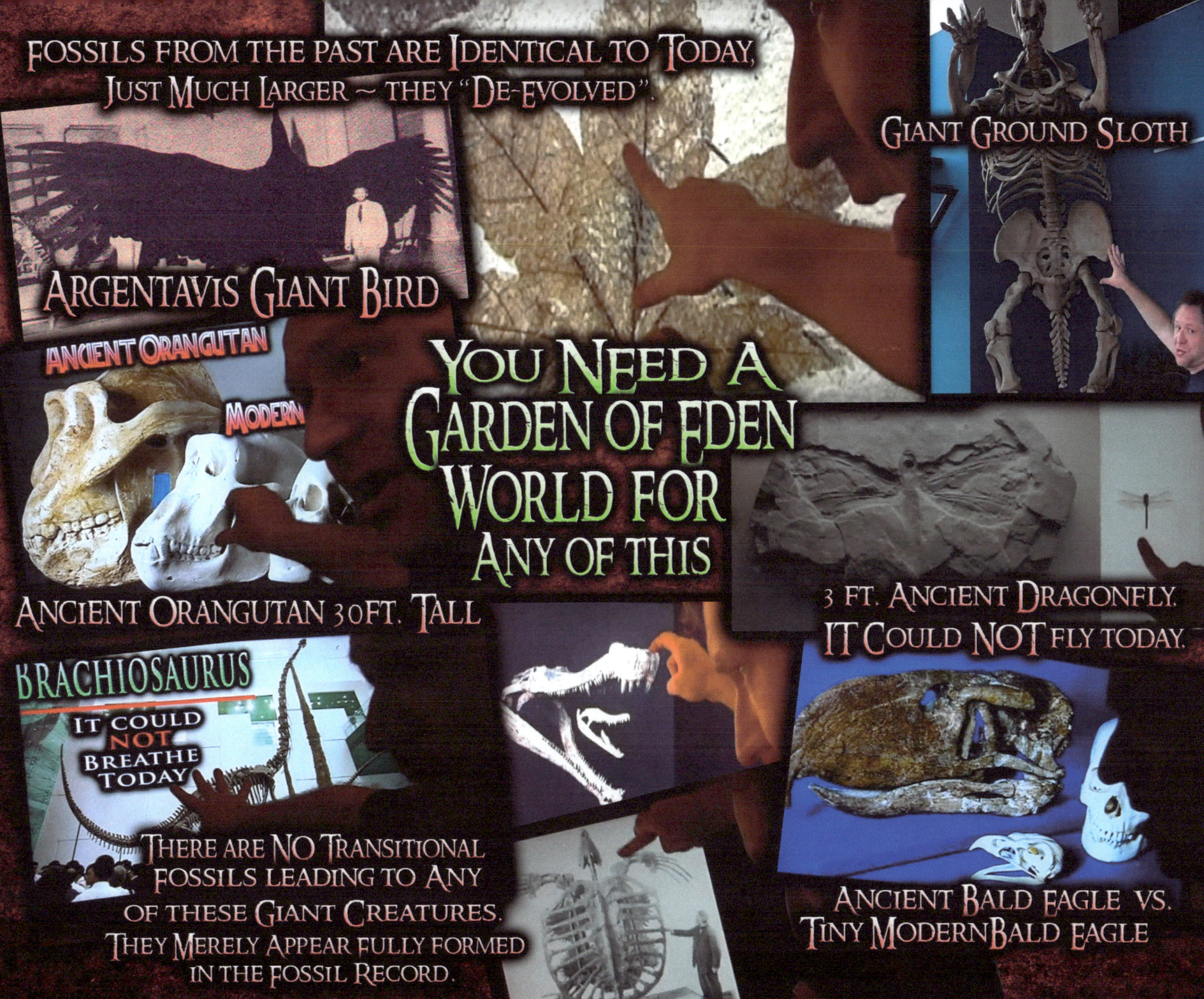

Ancient DragonFly

This Giant DragonFly could not lift off the ground to fly or breathe in today's atmosphere.

Modern DragonFly

Air bubbles trapped in fossilized tree resin show that the Pre-Flood world had double (at least) the Oxygen Levels of today.

It is claimed the Grand Canyon was formed over millions of years by the tiny Colorado River. If that were true, the entirety of the Colorado River should be a "Grand Canyon" ~ yet it's not.

In 1980, when Mount St. Helens volcano erupted, it melted a glacier. The water from that glacier raced as a flood and formed in minutes what is called "the Mini-Grand Canyon." The Grand Canyon is actually one of the "Grandest" evidences of the Global Flood.

Speaking of Mount St. Helens, the lava dome was Radioisotope dated following the eruption. It dated 340,000 ~ 2.4 million years old. The material should have shown an age of roughly 10 years old at the time of the test.

ARCHAEOLOGIST
DR. AARON JUDKINS
STANDS IN DINO / HUMAN
TRACKS IN
GLEN ROSE, TEXAS

14 HUMAN FOOTPRINTS WITH DINOSAUR /// FOOTPRINTS

THESE TRACKS WERE
DETERMINED
AUTHENTIC
BY THE DALLAS, TEXAS
POLICE CRIME LAB.

✓ CT VERIFIED

HUMAN FOOTPRINT WITH DINO TRACK

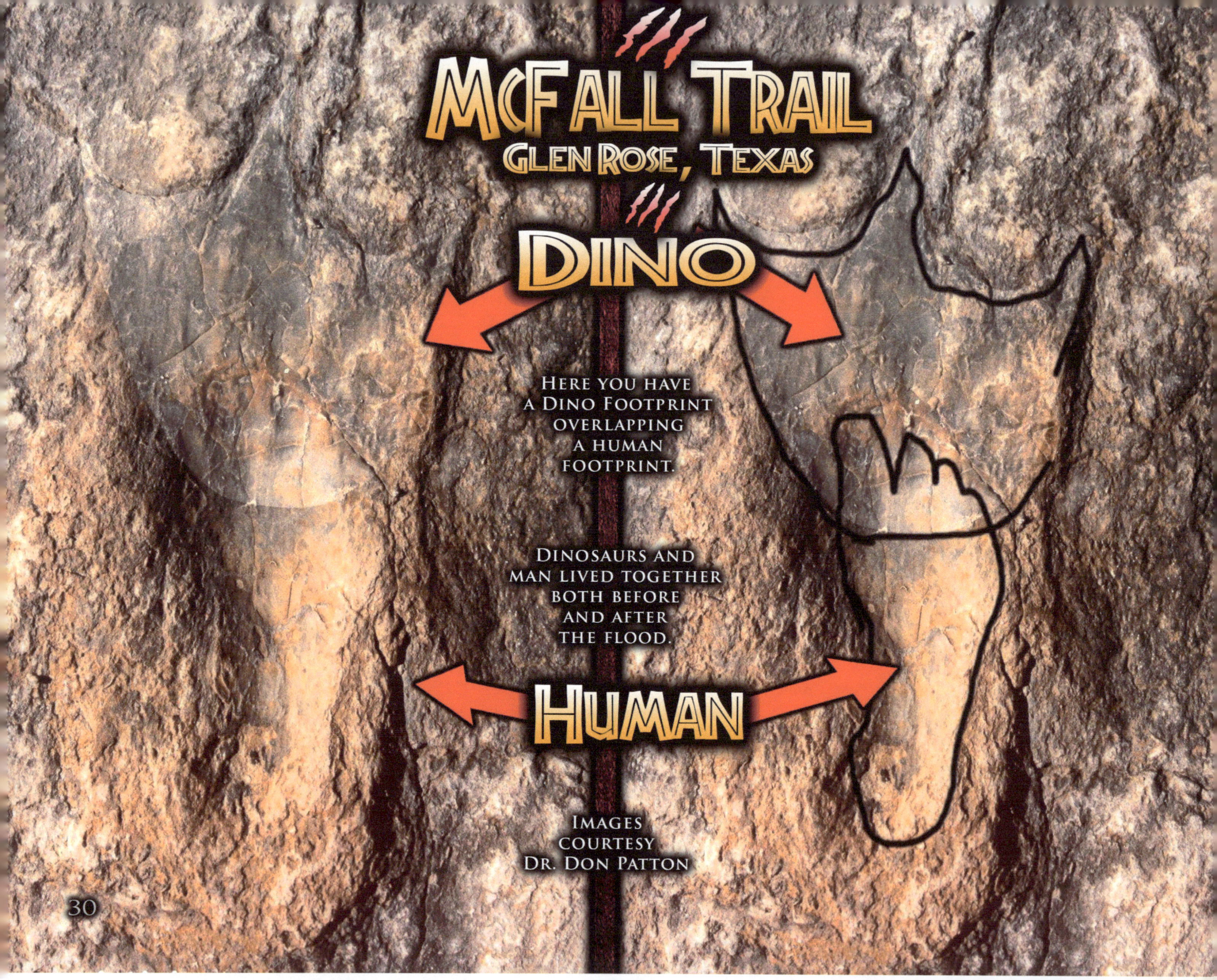

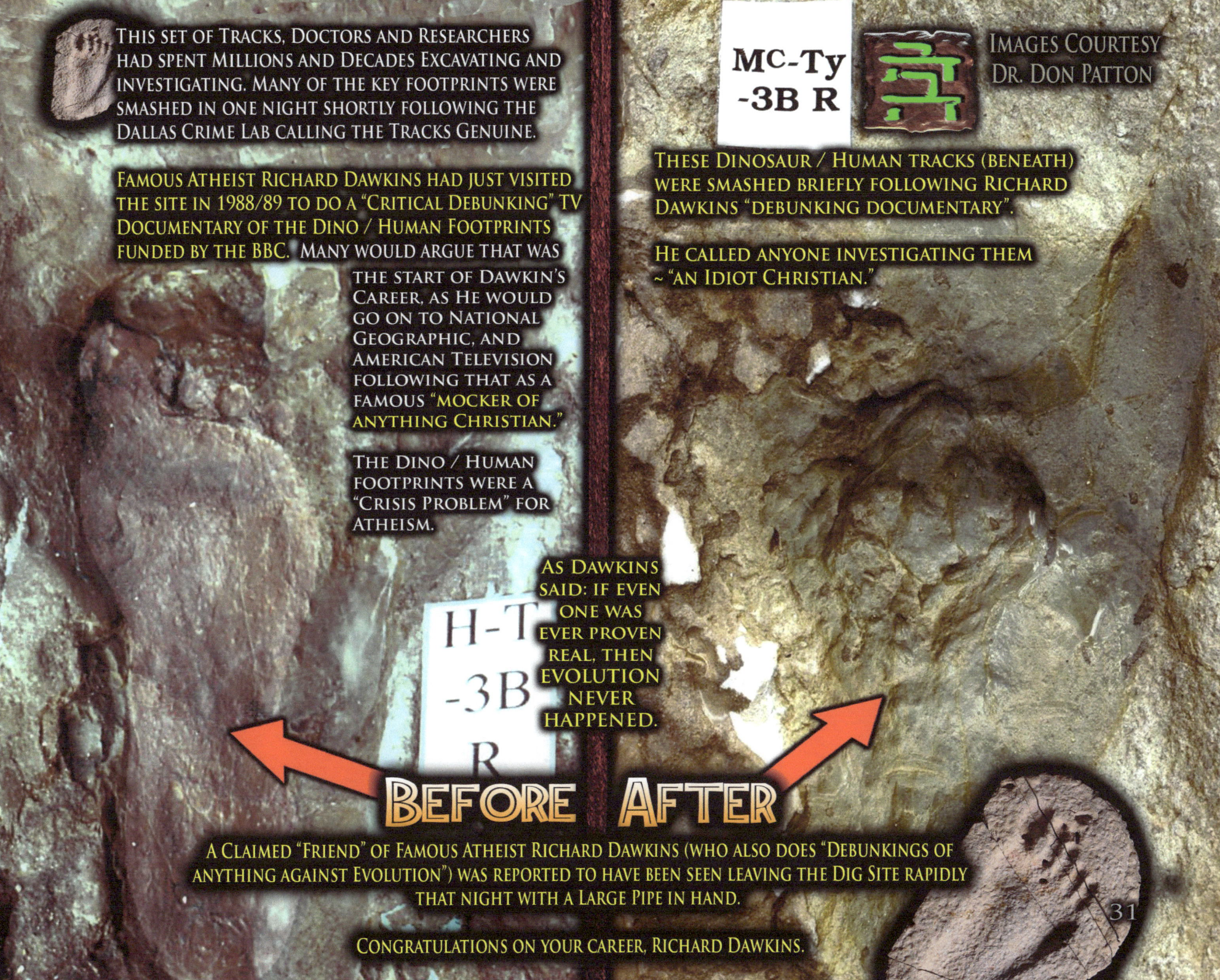

Mark Armitage is seen above holding a piece of Triceratops, who appeared in Trey Smith's "Jurassic," was fired after building the "Multimillion Dollar microscope Labs" for California State University.

He had released & published DATA in scientific journals on roughly a Half Dozen Dinosaurs, indicating they were "Young" (meaning well under 10,000 yrs. old). The University was charged with firing him for this, and destroying his reputation in science. All he did was provide imagery of living dinosaur cells and tissues.

The University later settled for what is reported a half million dollars.

Charles Lyell (an Attorney friend of Darwin) came up with the Geological Column. He believed that the different Layers (Strata) of Dirt represented "Time Periods."

Only Dirt doesn't sort like that...

It doesn't Lay down Limestone for a Million Years, then Decide....
Now I am Doing Sandstone...

It is Sorted Underground by weights and densities....

To be Clear, It is sorted Exactly as water would sort Dirt and Rock...

In fact, this is such a Common occurrence, we have a Scientific name for it: Liquifaction.

And the Layers or Strata of that Sedimentary Rock are GLOBAL.

Sedimentary Rock actually by its very definition means "Rock Layed down by Water."

The Animals and Creatures Cataclysmically Buried in those Layers are sorted by their Ecological Systems.

95% of your Fossil Record is Sea Life, Sea Shells, Plankton, and Clams. As would be the case if there were a Major Global Marine Catastrophy.

CHARLES DARWIN

The Man who believed breeding monkeys makes People

Darwin was born a very rich kid from a Banker Family.

Charles Darwin's Mom and Dad paid for him to go to Oxford University where he took the easiest and laziest classes available. However, he did ultimately achieve a degree in Theology, a tough subject; but no Sciences or even Business. His family, percieving this not profitable and a waste of their money - used their resources and political connections to arrange for Charles Darwin to go on the "HMS Beagle (ship)" -- where at least his family would not have to be around, or worry of him, for five years.

The HMS Beagle was a Military ship (HMS means "Her Majesty's Ship"). In other words, he was literally the only man on board without a job. He was 22 years old.

When he returned, he used his family's banking money to express that he understood the world better than every man, woman and child that had ever lived before him, in a document titled: "Origin of Species."

In short, all of written history was wrong (per Darwin's view), and people were the products of monkey's breeding.

The Science Community (even of that day -- the 1840's) laughed at him. Some saying, "Charles, even a small child knows you can't breed monkeys and get people."

None-the-less, there were parties that took Darwin seriously. Those were: Karl Marx, Stalin & Adolf Hitler. Some of the Worst Horrors in human history have been done per Darwin's banker funded "Theory."

If God created man, then even the least of us is of infinite value; and those who would do evil to others are answerable to a Higher Court. Under Darwin's Theory, people are of ZERO value. They are biological accidents, you can "Do as thou Will" to them -- merely monkeys -- and the biggest monkey gets the banana.

Darwin died miserable, many say whilst reading the Book of Hebrews.

CHARLES LYELL
(AN ATTORNEY FRIEND OF DARWIN)

"HIS THEORIES DELIGHTED ME... IF PUSHED
AS FAR AS IT MUST GO...
WOULD PROVE THAT MEN MAY
HAVE COME FROM THE OURANG-OUTANG."
~ CHARLES LYELL

FROZEN MAMMOTH

ENTIRE GIANT ECOLOGICAL SYSTEMS AND GIANT PRE-FLOOD ELEPHANTS WE TODAY CALL "MAMMOTHS" ARE ARE FOUND FROZEN IN PLACE BY WATER WHILST STANDING UP.

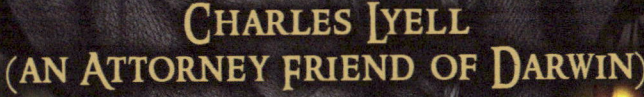

CLAIMED MISSING LINK "JAVA MAN"

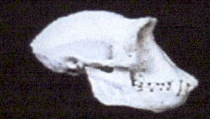 

MODERN CHIMPANZEE   ANCIENT CHIMPANZEE

MEANWHILE, OTHER CREATURES, SUCH AS THESE DINOSAURS IN MONGOLIA, ARE FOUND BURIED IN EARTH AND SLUDGE WHILST IN MID-BATTLE.

LITTLE DID LYELL KNOW THAT NOT ONLY WERE ANCIENT (PRE-FLOOD) OURANG-OUTANG'S 30 FT. TALL; BUT THEIR "MISSING LINK" JAVA MAN WOULD TURN OUT TO BE A GIANT CHIMPANZEE.

9 Warriors with Dinosaur

Amazon Rainforest, Peru
Image Courtesy Vance Nelson

Living dinos have been reported in the Amazon over the years.

MUŠHUŠŠU

The Mushuššu is a scaly dragon with a serpent like head. The depiction here is from the walls of Babylon, on the Ishtar gate.

Nebuchadnezar was the King at the time of Babylonian Captivity of Israel, and also the King under whom Daniel famously in his "Prophecy of Seventy Weeks" which predicted the exact day Jesus Christ would ride the donkey through the front gate of Jerusalem fullfilling Zechariah 9:9.

Nebuchadnezar wrote: "I (Nebuchadnezzar) laid the foundation of the gates down to the ground water level and had them built out of pure blue stone. Upon the walls in the inner room of the gate are bulls and dragons and thus I magnificently adorned them with luxurious splendor for all mankind to behold in awe."

Dragons (Dinosaurs) were perceived as regular animals in those times. They were, however, much smaller than many of their Mammoth Ancient versions found tangled in the great flood deposits and "dinosaur graveyards" we find underground.

Mushuššu was said to be a Pet of Marduk. And, the Babylonian god "Marduk" is likely the defied "Wicked Son" Mardon (per Book of Jasher) of Nimrod. His pet was a dinosaur/dragon.

SIR RICHARD OWEN

God said to the serpent: "Because you have done this, you are cursed more than all cattle, and more than every beast of the field; on your belly you shall go, and you shall eat dust all the days of your life. And I will put enmity between you and the woman, and between your seed and her seed; He shall bruise your head, and you shall bruise His heel." (Genesis 3:13-15)

Richard Owen lived from 1804 to 1892. He coined the word "Dinosaur" ~ meaning "Terrible Lizard." It was merely a scientific term "Dinosauria" to replace the word "Dragon."

He is seen here with a giant Ancient Moa, the mammoth ancient form of the modern ostrich.

Everything from the ancient past was BIGGER and BADDER than today. In fact, genetically, everthing here is weakening over time ~ de-evolving.

You see species go extinct, but not new ones arise.

To the left is an Ancient Snake fossilized. You can see he still had legs, The snake has genetically lost them over time.

Sir Richard Owen came up with the word "Dinosaur" ~ which is now used as the claimed proof of evolution. Richard Owen fought Darwin for most all of his life.

Tetrapodophis (Ancient Snake) photo by Ghedoghedo

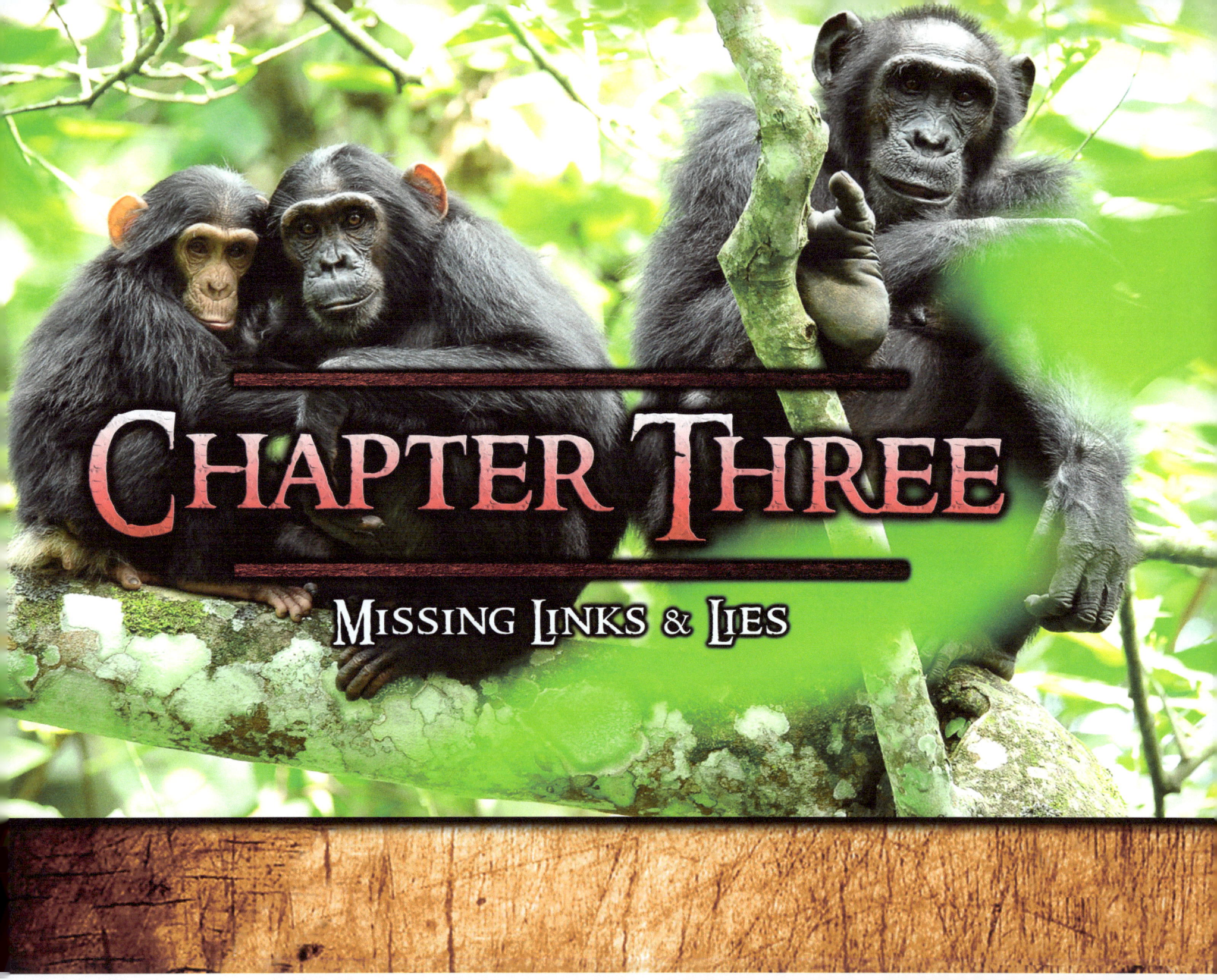

Chapter Three

Missing Links & Lies

Missing Link Lies

Claimed Missing Link "Piltdown man" skull being examined. Painting by John Cooke, 1915

Piltdown Man is what got evolution taught in Public Schools.
It was the first claimed "Missing Link."
It was later discovered to be fraud.

PILTDOWN MAN

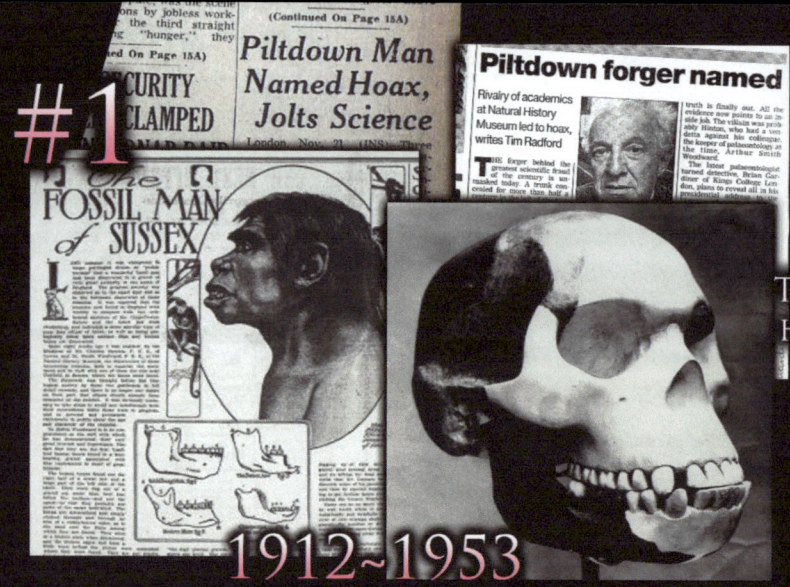

This is considered the first claimed missing link in human history. To claim evolution was true ~ they needed a Planet of the Apes style monkey-man.

This fraud lasted 40 years.

The claim was that if Christians were allowed to examine it, they would destroy it.

1912~1953

But, it came to the science communities attention than in 40 years of searching, no other one had ever been found. So, after 40 years, and upon examining the skull, it was determined to be a human head with an orangutan jaw attached.

Despite Piltdown man being fraud, it did get evolution taught in the public schools.

NEBRASKA MAN

Evolution supporters and funders claim Nebraska Man was a "better missing link" as it was not "deliberate fraud" ~ but rather, "just serious science error" on their part.

Nebraska Man was entirely constructed (in the marketing image to the right) from one tooth. The tooth turned out to be from an ancient pig ~ Not Bigfoot or a monkey-man.

1922

JAVA MAN

claimed "Homo erectus"

Java Man was "discovered" by Eugène Dubois, who was also one of the most hard-core Charles Darwin fans of the time. In fact, Dubois was as "hard-core" a Darwin Fan as Ernst Haeckel, who during the same time-frame produced the now infamous "Fraud Embryo" drawings to support Darwin's evolution.

Java Man was given the name "Pithecanthropus erectus" to make what would otherwise be called "the search for Bigfoot" sound scientific.

Pithecanthropus erectus is a fancy five dollar word for "erect ape-man" (which does notably sound better than "missing Planet of the Monkey Men").

Java man was comprised of parts found on the island of Java.

Though technically "discovered" before Piltdown Man, even evolutionists did not take it very seriously until after they knew for certain their other examples (Piltdown & Nebraska) were entirely bogus.

Today, evolutionists call Java Man, "Homo Erectus."

Additionally, even hard-core Darwin lovers of this modern age concede that Dubois was later found to have stashed many animal and human bones in his home.

The leg bone is clearly human for Java man. Whereas, the skullcap (as Dubois himself points out) appears to clearly belong to an ancient chimpanzee.

He claims he found the parts at different times.

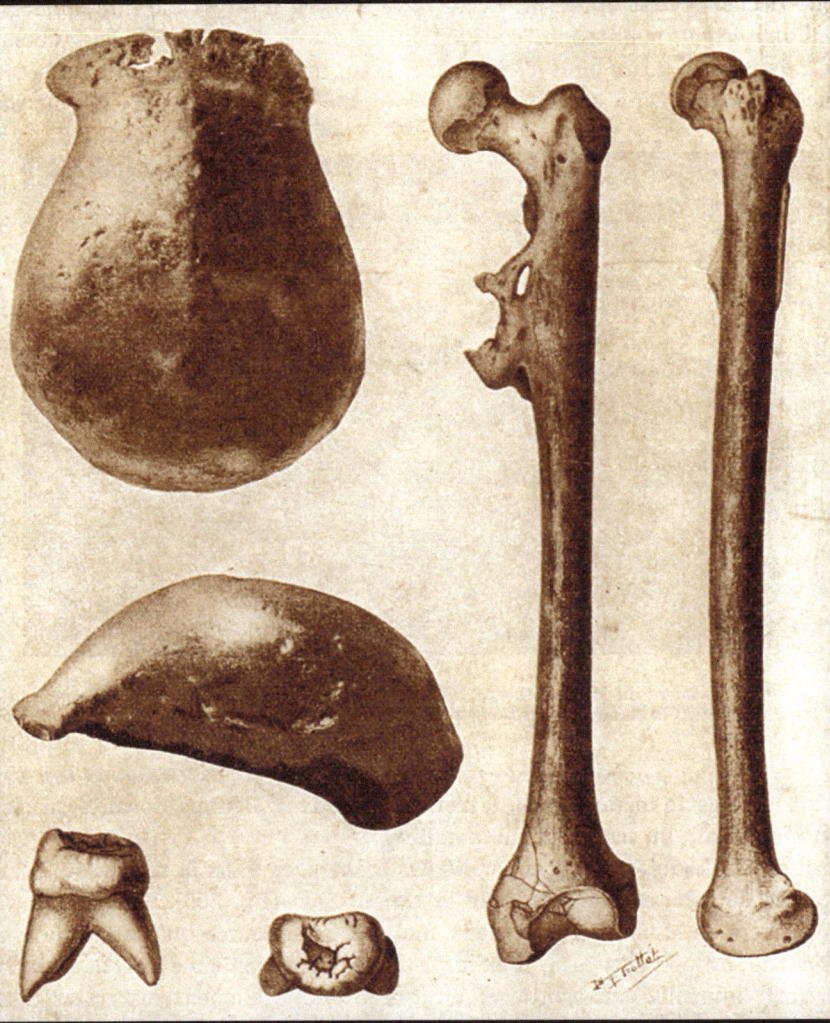

1891

Humans have a forehead. Monkeys (primates) have no forehead.

DMANISI MAN

another claimed "Homo erectus"

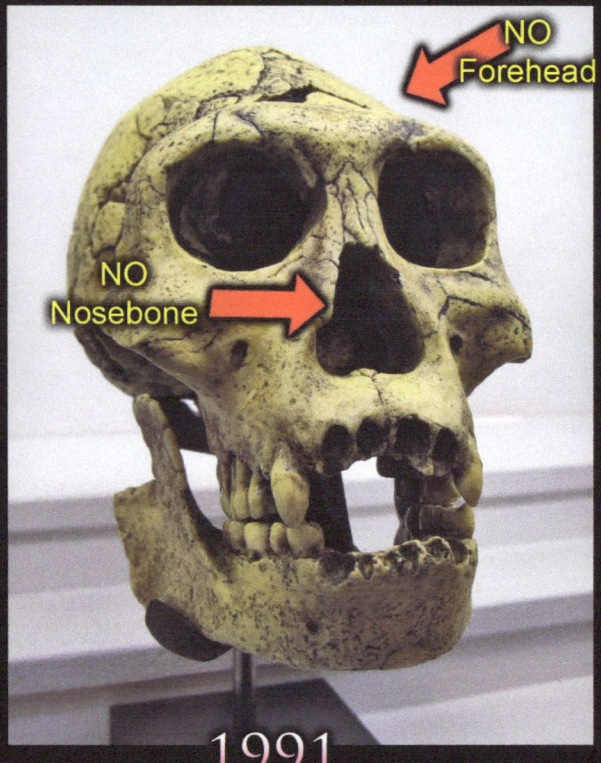

NO Forehead

NO Nosebone

1991

Evolution had become so well funded, that any ape-skull (like the one to the left) could be called a missing link and marketed to the public by claimed "(Grant-Funded) experts." Though many would argue this has tarnished the once stellar value of universities, and the students attending therein, in favor of a 150 year old "Theory of a monkey world" by a 22 year old rich kid named Darwin ~ it does serve as a way for us today to clearly understand the simple and straight-forward differences between monkeys and humans.

Dmansi man is one of five ape skulls found among 3000 ancient animal fossils ~ including ancient rhinos, ancient horses, and ancient giant cats.

It is an ancient ape.

TAUTAVEL MAN

another claimed "Homo erectus"

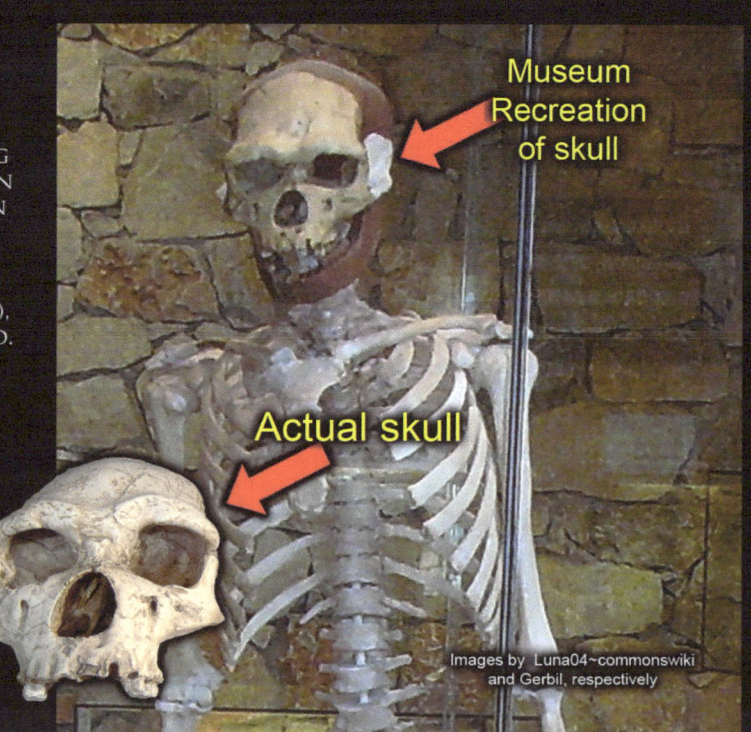

Museum Recreation of skull

Actual skull

Homo Erectus is the classification under which evolutionists began mixing human skulls and monkey skulls under the same label ~ in a slicker way than the unfunded methods that started it all with the pure fraud of Piltdown man.

As you can see in the top left is clearly an ape (primate) as primates have NO nose bone, NOR forehead. Yet, under the same classification (Homo Erectus), the skull (recreation) of Tautavel man has a nose bone and a giant forehead.

Notice on Tautavel man (to left) that the recreation to market to the public is far different from the real skull. The recreation has a giant forehead, the actual skull does not (primate forehead). The recreation has a hint sufficient to be called a nose bone, the actual skull looks monkey all the way.

And, it is not just one or two examples of this kind of clear misrepresentation; with evolution ~ misrepresentation is the name of the game.

Images by Luna04~commonswiki and Gerbil, respectively

Neanderthal Man

La Chapelle-aux-Saints 1

Early Neanderthal skulls were very often released to the public with missing nose bones, like the La Chapelle skull to the right. Removing the nose bone can make a human skull look "monkey-like (primate)." However, over time too many skulls were found and not all could be removed.

Neanderthals were drawn and covered with modeling clay to look as monkey men.

Neanderthals are ancient humans, bone-for-bone.

In fact, not only were they not monkey men, but like everything in the ancient world (particularly before the flood), they were thicker, far stronger, had larger brains, and lived far longer than we do today.

Also, they were far better looking and more physically fit than we could dream of.

We are a dimished version of our fathers and ancestors that lived much before us.

Much effort from evolutionist went into making these ancient ancestors, such as the likes of Nimrod, Noah, Enoch or Adam, and the sons and daughters and generations thereof, look like primates.

The skull on the bottom right is what a Neanderthal skull actually looks like (with the nose bone intact).

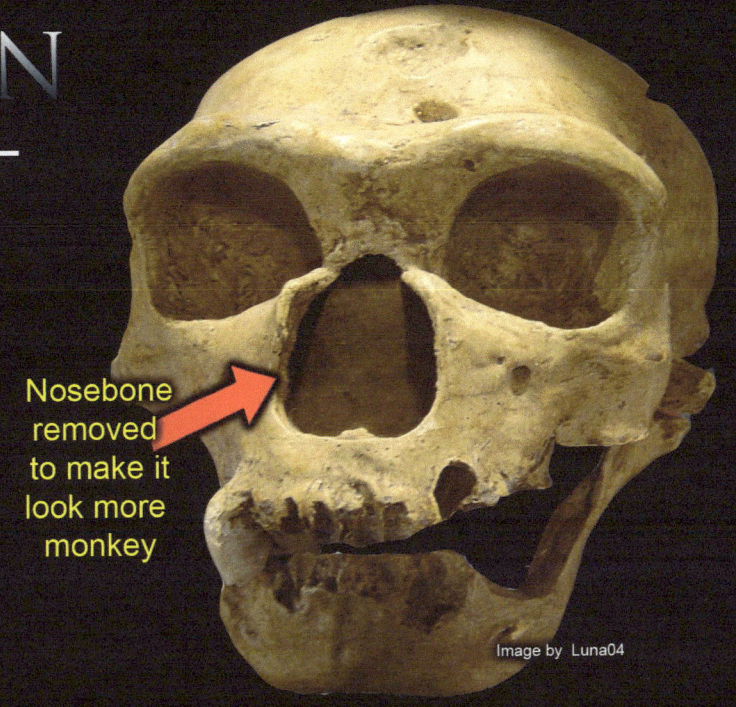

Nosebone removed to make it look more monkey

Image by Luna04

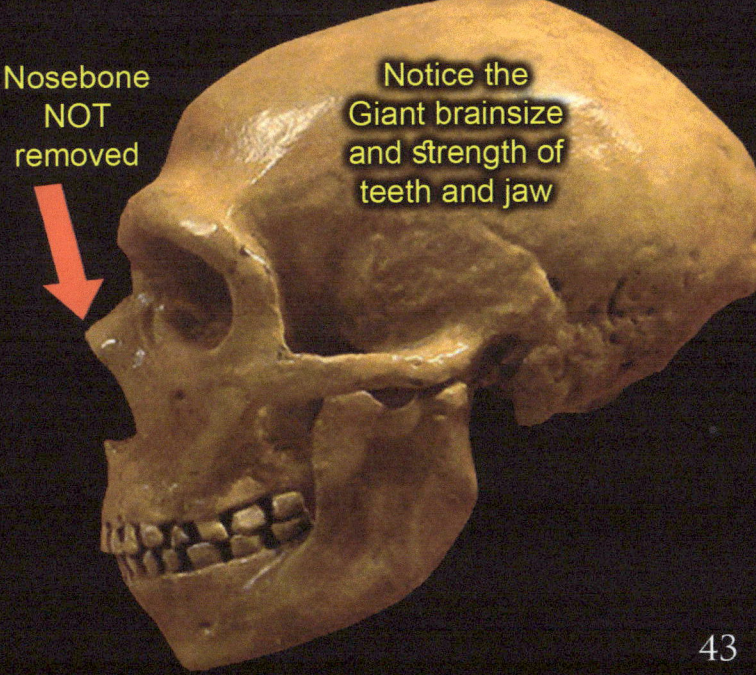

Nosebone NOT removed

Notice the Giant brainsize and strength of teeth and jaw

NEANDERTHALS

Our Ancestors from the Very Start of Man Kind....

Cranial features of Modern Man and Neanderthal compared

- BRAINCASE SHAPE
- FOREHEAD
- BROWRIDGE
- NASAL BONE PROJECTION
- CHEEK BONE ANGULATION
- "BUN"
- CHIN
- OCCIPITAL CONTOUR

Neanderthals are Bone for Bone Human Skeletons....
The Only Differences are that the Bones are Thicker, Stronger, more Durable, the Wisdom Teeth fit Perfectly,

and, The Brain Sizes Are Much Larger.

They are simply Ancient Heavy Duty Human Skeletons. Not Dissimilar to the "Heavy Duty" Garden of Eden Style Animals We find from the Past.

As if We Today are the Degenerated, much Weaker, Version of Our Ancestors.

NEANDERTHALS

CARBON DATE THE SAME AGE AS DINOSAURS AND WOOLY MAMMOTHS

IMAGE OF NEANDERTHAL NATIONAL MUSEUM OF NATURE AND SCIENCE, TOKYO.

CREDIT この利用者は日本語の母語話者です。

OUR ANCESTORS, COMING FROM ADAM AND EVE...... EXTRA LONG LIFE SPANS.

DR. JACK CUOZZO

IN 1977, HE STUDIED IN SWITZERLAND WITH DR. FRANCIS SCHAEFFER AND IN 1979, BEGAN MUCH OF THE ORIGINAL STUDY OF NEANDERTHAL FOSSILS.

HE WAS (AND IS TODAY) ONE OF THE FOREMOST EXPERTS ON NEANDERTHALS; PARTICULALRY JUVENILE NEANDERTHALS.

HE BECAME A CLAIMED "CONTROVERSIAL FIGURE" AS HE LATER CLAIMED THOSE IN SUPPORT OF GRANT FUNDING MONEY FOR EVOLUTION HAD BEEN ALTERING (OR DESTROYING) SKULLS IN EFFORTS TO MAKE THEM "MORE APE-LIKE."

DR CUOZZO BECAME ONE OF THE FIRST TO ARGUE WHAT IS COMMON KNOWLEDGE TODAY ~ THAT "NEANDERTHAL" WAS JUST A FANCY WORD FOR ANCIENT HUMANS LIKE US.

FURTHER HOWEVER, CUOZZO DEMONSTRATED THAT NEANDERTHALS DID HAVE "UNUSUAL TRAITS" ~ THEY APPEARED TO LIVE EXCESSIVELY LONGER LIVES THAN MODERN HUMANS TODAY. HE ARGUED THE BONES SHOWED THEY LIVED FOR HUNDREDS AND HUNDREDS OF YEARS (IN MANY CASES).

CUOZZO ALSO SHOWED THAT IN YOUNG NEANDERTHALS THEY TOOK VERY LONG TIMES TO REACH "ADULTHOOD" ~ A PERSON THE AGE OF 40 MIGHT BE JUST ENDING PUBERITY.

ADDITIONALLY, CUOZZO PRESENTED IN HIS BOOK "BURIED ALIVE" THAT MANY (OR MOST) NEANDERTHALS DIED BY MASSIVE DROWNING.

BURIED ALIVE — Jack Cuozzo
Never-Before-Seen Photos
HIDDEN, SUFFOCATING FROM THE PAIN OF A STORY LEFT UNTOLD...
The Startling Truth About Neanderthal Man

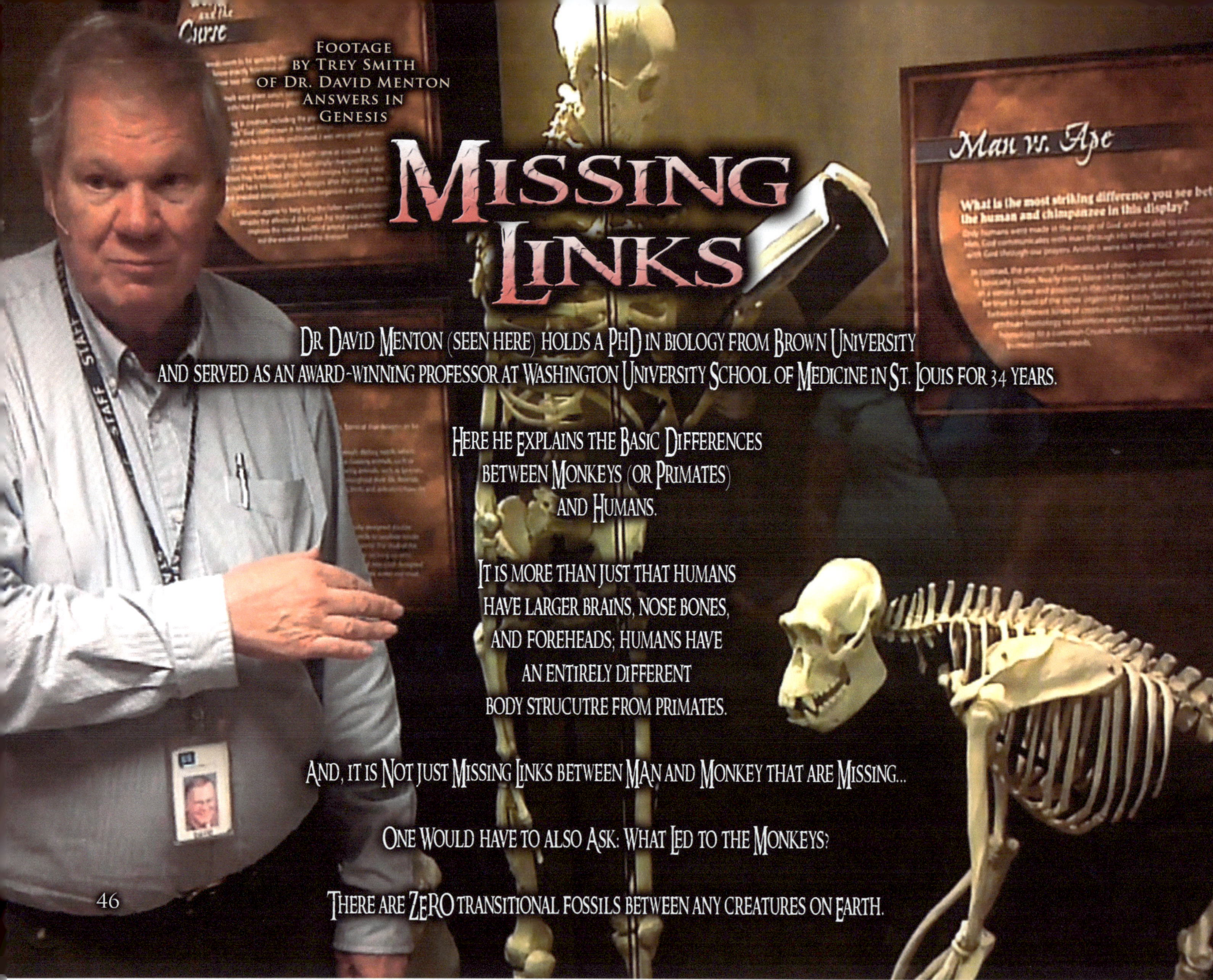

Missing Links

Footage by Trey Smith of Answers in Genesis "Lucy"

Footage by Trey Smith Ozark Museum & Giant ancient Mammoth (Elephant)

Lucy

Is the most famous of the claimed "Missing Links" over time. She is likely also the last to ever be taken very serioulsy.

Lucy was a common ancient Chimpanzee.

To the right is how "Lucy" has been depicted over the years; like a little "monkey-person". Lucy "Promoters" argued that if they just had the "Missing Parts" this is how she looked.

Many "Lucys" have been found over the past 40 years. There are NO LONGER "Missing Parts" to argue.

Congratulations, the Discoverers found a Dead Monkey in Africa.

47

PILLARS OF CREATION

CHAPTER FOUR

TIME

IMAGE CREATED BY NASA

EYE OF GOD NEBULA

Your Greatest Minds have called it the Largest mystery

TIME

Therefore let us explain it in a very simple few pages

Image Created by NASA

Eye of God Nebula

Image Created by NASA

I state "Image created by NASA" because as I write this page there is a war over the credibility in sciences. What I mean by that, is that sciences in general are becoming less "science" and more "fiction".

None-the-less, the images are beautiful. Accordingly, NASA itself appears to essentially state:

When Hubble beams down images, astronomers have to make many adjustments, such as adding color and patching multiple photos together, to that raw data before the space observatory's images are released to the public.

Hubble doesn't use color film (or any film at all) to create its images. "We often use color as a tool, whether it is to enhance an object's detail or to visualize what ordinarily could never be seen by the human eye,"

Trey's Notes:

For all these reasons and more, we will focus not on the universe, but on things closer to home ~ beginning with TIME. ~Trey

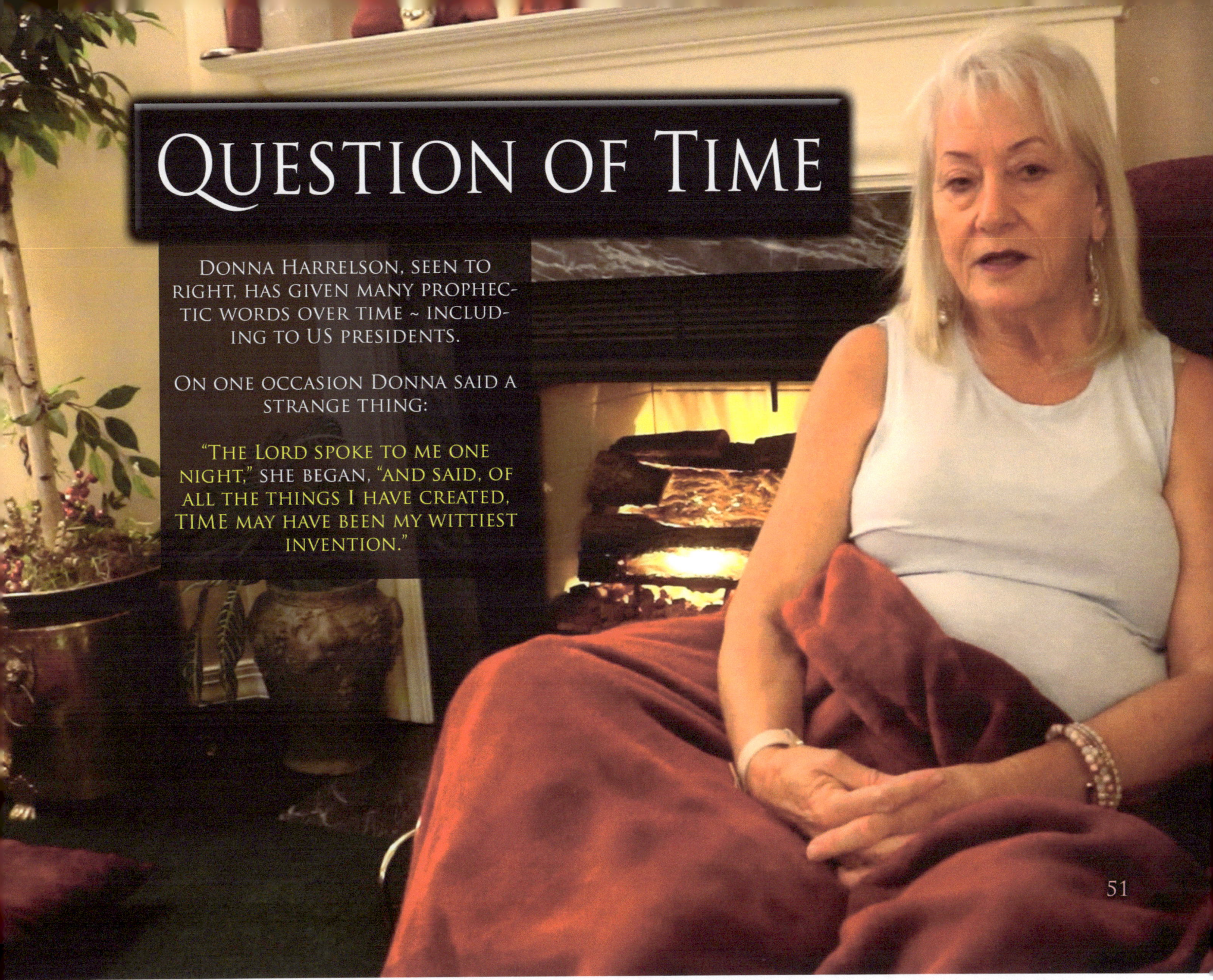

QUESTION OF TIME

Donna Harrelson, seen to right, has given many prophetic words over time ~ including to US presidents.

On one occasion Donna said a strange thing:

"The Lord spoke to me one night," she began, "and said, of all the things I have created, time may have been my wittiest invention."

51

REALITY IN CIRCLES

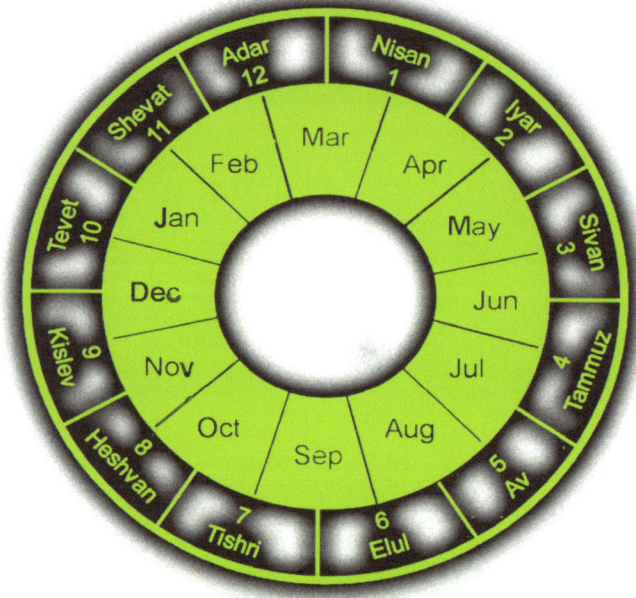

Strangely, reality in this place works much a test environment on a computer.

This begins with the fact you are isolated in giant void of space with 8 planets, like hands on a big clock going in precision circles within. And, everything outside of those 8 planets is too far for you to ever dream to reach. This applies whether you believe stars are other suns, or something else.

Additionally, you are going in circles in time, within that vast void of space ~ like a very large scratch pad in a programmer's test environment.

Accordingly, a "test environment" always has a "tester" ~ otherwise it would not be a test.

Above is the 12 months of the years in Hebrew, Enoch and the Gregorian calendar.

They go in circles, just as do your weeks in 7 day cycles, and also your seasons.

No matter what calendar you use, you are always going round and round.

You are always coming back to where you first began.

Above is the geocentric model of the universe from 1539 AD. It has the Earth as the center stage of the stars, sun and planets.

What is interesting, is that whether you use the ancient models, or our modern models (with the sun in the middle) ~ the further you go, the closer you are to where you first began.

Also, the stars are too far for you to ever reach on your own ~ by design.

Further up the Spiral

It is commonly said that those in support of young Darwin's Theory of Evolution would use circular reasoning to get the "deep time" dates they needed for the theory to work. **This is true.** They would use the rocks to give the claimed age of the fossils, and then turn around and use the fossils to give the claimed date of the rocks ~ so it would sound "scientific" whilst giving dates based on pure imagination.

In the example below, we have fish fossilized so rapidly they didn't have time to swallow the fish they were eating. All fossils are sorted by ecological systems, in the same way a global water catastrophy would sort dirt, stone, and biological creatures ~ this is also why there are trilobytes, and giant earthworms at the bottom.

Taking this a step further, everything here is circular. For example, if you were asked to "scientifically" describe a tree ~ **you would use a tree to describe a tree. It is a paradox.**

A created thing can never understand the full scope of it's Creator.

And, there is NO WAY for us to describe the dimensions above us ~ the place from which this place comes from. We can only describe reality as it has been presented. In short, you were simply birthed right out of thin air into this reality ~ you did not choose this place, the game, or the rules therein ~ but make no mistake about it: While you are alive, you are a player on the board.

Most people go their entire lives without asking the three questions that matter most: **Who am I? Where did I come from? What happens next?** These are the same three questions one would ask if they woke up in a ditch.

You will find that everything here is a paradox ~ just like describing a tree by using a tree. And, the tree is actually made of dirt, constructed into reality by the precision coding preprogrammed in the seed.

You would use a Tree to describe a Tree. It is a Paradox.

You also can NOT get the tree without the seed; nor can you get the seed without the tree. There is no chicken before the egg. It is a paradox ~ and the coding has to be complete from the start.

TESSERACT

A Tesseract is a fourth-dimensional object (cube) unfolded into a three-dimensional space. The fourth dimensional tesseract unfolds into a cross of cubes ~ just as a cube (three dimensional) unfolds into a two-dimensional cross.

The full Tesseract can not be seen, as it is a "Higher Dimensional" object; only the geometric edges which unfold into our Three Dimensional reality ~ which happens to form a cross ~ can be seen. The gate.

In Salvador Dali's famous painting (top left), the cross is literally an unseen dimensional doorway kissing with our reality ~ literally the narrow gate between worlds.

A Three Dimensional Cube (or Box) unfolds into six Squares ~ just as man was created on the Sixth day. The unfolded cube (to Right) is now a Two Dimensional object ~ a lower Dimensional Object than our reality.

The Vav (number six) is literally imbedded in the 3 letter name of God (making 4 letters total). The Rabbis claim the Vav ~ the number and symbol of man ~ is the only letter connecting Heaven to Earth.

Crucifixion
Corpus Hypercubus
1954 ~ Salvador Dalí

Always watch the signs & shadows

Cube (Box)
Unfolds into a cross
It is a cross of Six Squares

He 5   Vav 6   He 5   Yod 10

YHVH (above) means "Behold Hand, Behold Nail". The Nail, holding the hands to the cross, is also the number (6) six.

Tom and Sally are Two Dimensional Stick people. They are on a lower Dimension than our Three Dimensional world. For this reason, they could never understand our world.

In fact, as their creator, I could come face-to-face with Tom and Sally ~ yet they would never know I was even there. If I were to pass a 3-dimensional ball through their world, they would only see a circle ~ or a line getting bigger then smaller before magically vanishing.

Greater still, Tom cannot even see Sally the way she is ~ he only sees a straight line when he looks at her.

What then does our Creator, in a dimension larger than we could ever understand, see when He looks at us?

Quantum Particles

It is said that Quantum Particles (sub-atomic Particles smaller than atoms) which are the Matrix of Everything in our 3-Dimensional Reality ~ break ALL the RULES of standard Physics ~ creating measurement problems in abundance. And, making a Unified Theory of Everything impossible.

The reason for this is simple.

When you are doing measurements, even of this place's smallest parts ~ you are already looking at the past.

When you are staring at the Quantum Particles of this place ~ you are Looking at the precise spot & moment where Reality becomes.

Of course it breaks all the rules.

When you are looking at a two dimensional screen, it is made of Tiny Pixels ~ just as our Three dimensional Reality is made of Tiny Particles.

When you are looking at a person on a screen (our modern crystal balls) ~ you are NOT seeing that person; but rather, an illusion of that person, an avatar ~ made of little pixels of synthetic light.

The image on the screen is actually made of highly organized and programmed data, which your eyes cannot see, and can flow right through your fingers in the thin air.

Yet, there is no question it is the source feeding the data and illusions on the screen.

Reality, as your eyes are designed to perceive it, is 99.9% empty space ~ an illusion of those tiny subatomic particles appearing wherever they need to appear next, to make up the matrix of this material world we call "Reality."

Image is an illusion of non-random pixels; just as "reality" is made of "particles" ~ and YOU (the observer) are also made of those same particles ~ meaning YOU can NOT see "beyond the looking glass."

Just as the Data fed to your TV, laptop or phone is coming from a non-Random, intelligent source ~ Reality itself, and all those little particle-pixels making the matrix thereof, causing the science guys to go both sideways and silly ~ is indeed **coming from an INCOMPREHENSIBLY LARGER INTELLIGENT SOURCE.**

The pixels are fed by an invisible source. At the moment the "invisible data" becomes the "visible image" ~ it creates (a subset of) "Time."

This is why Quantum Particles are measured in probabilies ~ You can NOT determine exactly where they will appear next. And, when you have non-random data appearing out of thin air as tiny dots, the next question should always be: What is the Source?

In this instance, the answer is LARGER THAN the IMAGINATION.

And, the particles are breaking all the rules ~ because the "program (Reality)" is interactive.... Those particles have to make provision for whatever YOU, or any other "player on the board" may do next.

As a side effect, at that: "moment reality becomes" ~ just as when you press play on your DVD player and the data becomes moving images on your screen ~ it has just become a synthetic subset of time.

In short, Time is the product of that instant of translation. And, Time is measurable by the Planck second and the Quantum Constant.

As straight-forward as this otherwise seems ~ with NO continuum of data stream, there is NO image, NO reality. It really is that simple.

Some argue: God could not have created the World & Universe in Six Days; whilst the sciences in the very palm of your hand are screaming that EVERY PARTICLE of this Illusion is recreated and maintained millions of times a second.

TIME

Everything here in the material world is made of Atoms, going back all the way to Adam.

Those atoms are 99.9% empty space.

You and everything here really are an illusion.

Atoms are dancing vibrations of Light and Energy. So, the matrix of reality is in truth a musical song.

Creation itself glorifies its Creator. Men speak words, perhaps God Himself speaks substance.

It was with words that these worlds were formed.

Atoms are made of smaller particles.

The Particles making up Atoms ~ which make the Matrix of Reality ~ are a continuous stream.

Those particles in the Quantum World have to break all the rules as they are creating "reality" in "Real Time" ~ this is how time itself is generated.

You are living in tiny subset of much larger and far more complex reality ~ which is precisely what the ancient pages of your Bible have been telling you.

Imagine if you could hit the computer keyboard "show code key" on reality ~ what would you see?

Consciousness

Your physical body as well as the matrix of the 3-dimensional construct of reality around you, are moving through time at a rate Max Planck measured as 10^{-43} seconds.

Within that "time" and inside that "contruct of Reality" ~ you are conscious.

Conciousness is what is allowing you to experiance "Reality."

So, in a very "real" sence:

You are "birthed" into a reality that behaves much like an intensely complex computer program. You are built from DNA, that acts and is identical to software ~ and constructs YOU into this place from scratch. And, as the red cherry heart ontop ~ you are consciously plugged into this place as if by WI-FI.

That's one heck of a mud puddle coming to life.

The body is like a vessel (a machine) ~ a space suit built for this place ~ and the mind is recording all of it. Which also means: all thoughts have an origin (Good & Evil alike). It also means your entire life could, can & will be played back like a DVD before God.

And one more thing: This also raises the question of where you "really" even are as you sit to read this page. Ephesians says you are already "seated in heavenly places."

BIG BANG

The Big Bang Theory was created as an "add-on" for the Theory of Evolution. If monkeys had become people, and the monkeys came from mud puddles hit by lightning bolts (actual theory) that had come to life ~ then surely the Universe and every precision thing within it could come from nowhere.

The name "Big Bang" comes from English astronomer and cosmologist Sir Fred Hoyle, who was in 1949 making fun of the theory.

Hoyle spent a lot of his life fighting the Big Bang which was actually named by him ~ as comedy would have it.

In the Beginning there was NOTHING. Then it Exploded, and created Everything. If you'll believe that, you'll believe anything.

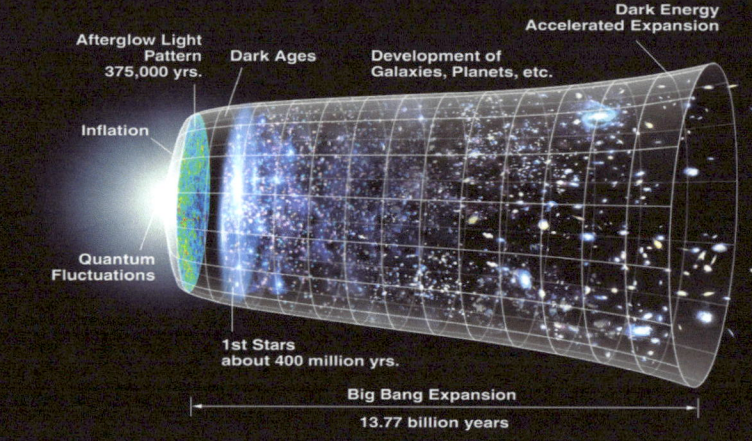

The image above is a model of the Big bang provided by NASA. Models can be made of anything. For example: Modeling clay can be put on a monkey skull to make it look like a great intellectual of Earth. Conversely, a human skull can be made by modeling to look as nothing more than a primative primate.

Accordingly, even a model that works on a computer screen does not make something "real" or "true" any more than the CGI special effects of a sci-fi film are real or true. Taking that a step further, I can say "one apple plus one apple is two apples" ~ yet it does not create the apples into "Reality."

The Big Bang has failed (and been the reverse of) literally hundreds of scientific predictions ~ Hours worth of the reasons the Big Bang could have NEVER happened are listed out comprehensively in simple, easy language by Denver, Colorado's Real Science Radio, Bob Enyart.

Its problems are larger than just the fine tuning of the Universe, and particularly our Solar System, appearing carefully designed by an Intelligent mind. Or, that the Universe is missing an entire Universe-worth of "magical" antimatter to make that fine tuning work like a crafted clock; or the fact that planets, the Sun, stars or moons could never form from a giant space explosion ~ but moreover ~ the only place the Big Bang actually works is in the CGI of a science fiction TV show.

SPACE

Another little known secret of space often brushed quietly under the rug is what some Atheists & Cosmologists have called ~ "The Axis of Evil."
This is a little like Nimrod from the Book of Jasher calling Abram "Evil" as his stargazers and witchy people had said a child (Abram) had been born that would destroy his works and empire.
What the Axis of Evil is: if you use the very data that was suppose to prove the Big Bang, Cosmic Microwave Background (CMB) radiation, you end up finding the "anomaly" that the Earth appears to be the center stage of the Universe. For the Athiest, this is "Evil".

While those vested in the rat-race of Darwinism assure me they are working hard and frantically for solutions to "Evil Problems" such as this ~ I would prefer to quote you from some of the greatest minds of both space and science.

One of my Father's friends, Don Sanders, had Top Secret clearance for NASA ~ and was awarded many government contracts following retirement ~ including at Wright-Patterson, where the aliens were alledgedly taken following Roswell. My Father wrote some of the security software for these places.

Another man, however, would be Wernher von Braun.

He worked directly for Adolf Hitler building rockets; and also, directly under President Kennedy building NASA. His very title was "Top Secret" by definition for two countries.

If we knew Von Braun's secrets ~ they would be beyond imagination. What we do know is that this is what the top-man in space science wanted as his last words in this place, to be printed on his tombstone ~ Psalms 19.

"The heavens declare the glory of God; and the firmament sheweth the work of His hands.

Day unto day the heavens uttereth speech, and night unto night the stars sheweth knowledge." ~ Psalms 19

THE BOOK OF GENESIS

CHAPTER FIVE

THE ANOMALIES EVERYWHERE

Otherwise known as the Book of "Genes~is"

Speaking of Time & Coding....

Perhaps we should
Look at some
Not so old things.

1947
CARBON DATING
INVENTED BY WILLARD LIBBY

"YOU READ BOOKS AND FIND STATEMENTS THAT SUCH AND SUCH A SOCIETY OR ARCHAEOLOGICAL SITE IS [CLAIMED TO BE] 20,000 YEARS OLD. WE LEARNED RATHER ABRUPTLY THAT THESE NUMBERS, THESE ANCIENT AGES, ARE NOT KNOWN (SPECULATIONS & IMAGINATIVE GUESSES). IN FACT, IT IS ABOUT THE TIME OF THE FIRST DYNASTY IN EGYPT THAT THE LAST [EARLIEST] HISTORICAL DATE OF ANY REAL CERTAINTY HAS BEEN ESTABLISHED."
~ WILLARD LIBBY

ON A NEWLY FORMED EARTH, FOR C-14 TO EQUALIZE IN THE ATMOSPHERE WOULD TAKE ABOUT 30,000 YEARS. TESTS SHOW THAT C-14 IS STILL INCREASING IN THE ATMOSPHERE....
IT HAS NOT EQUALIZED
IN LAYMEN'S TERMS, THE ATMOSPHERE IS NOT EVEN 30,000 YRS. OLD.

FURTHER STILL, IF THE ENTIRE EARTH WERE ONE BALL OF C-14, IT WOULD BE COMPLETELY GONE IN ONE MILLION YEARS.

YET, YOU FIND IT IN EVERYTHING FROM DINOSAURS TO DIAMONDS.

BUT, IT IS TRUE THAT YOUR PLANTS AND ANIMALS FROM THE PAST REQUIRED AN ENTIRELY DIFFERENT ECOLOGICAL SYSTEM....

BRACHIOSAURUS
IT COULD NOT BREATHE TODAY

THAT MEANS A DIFFERENT ATMOSPHERE...
INDEED, THAT WOULD KICK OUT
LARGE NUMBERS ON YOUR CARBON TESTS.

1947 Carbon Dating
Invented by Willard Libby

These Beneath are Actual Carbon Dating Results from Dinosaur Bones. These Results were Censored by Universities.

Wooly Mammoth Dates

Site	^{14}C years BP
Pyskowice	25,420 ± 210
Pyskowice	25,940 ± 230
Pyskowice	28,090 ± 280
Góra Winnica n.Kamień Mścic	28,190 ± 280
Krosinko	31,160 ± 390
Podgórze near Zawichost	32,150 ± 450
Pyzdry	40,000 ± 1200
Bydgoszcz Bielawy	41,500 ± 1400
Krosinko	43,800 ± 1900
Przewóz	48,600 ± 3500

One Vollosovitch Mammoth dated at both 29,000 yrs. and 44,000 yrs. at once.

The data: Carbon-14 in dinosaur bones

Dinosaur (a)	Lab/Method/Fraction (b,c,d)	C-14 Years B.P.	Date	USA State
Acro	GX-15155-A/Beta/bio	>32,400	11/10/1989	TX
Acro	GX-15155-A/AMS/bio	25,750 ± 280	06/14/1990	TX
Acro	AA-5786/AMS/bio-scrapings	23,760 ± 270	10/23/1990	TX
Acro	UGAMS-7509a/AMS/bio	29,690 ± 90	10/27/2010	TX
Acro	UGAMS-7509b/AMS/bow	30,640 ± 90	10/27/2010	TX
Allosaurus	UGAMS-02947/AMS/bio	31,360 ± 100	05/01/2008	CO
Hadrosaur #1	KIA-5523/AMS/bow	31,050 + 230/-220	10/01/1998	AK
Hadrosaur #1	KIA-5523/AMS/hum	36,480 + 560/-530	10/01/1998	AK
Triceratops #1	GX-32372/AMS/col	30,890 ± 200	08/25/2006	MT
Triceratops #1	GX-32647/Beta/bow	33,830 + 2910/-1960	09/12/2006	MT
Triceratops #1	UGAMS-04973a/AMS/bio	24,340 ± 70	10/29/2009	MT
Triceratops #2	UGAMS-03228a/AMS/bio	39,230 ± 140	08/27/2008	MT
Triceratops #2	UGAMS-03228b/AMS/col	30,110 ± 80	08/27/2008	MT
Hadrosaur #2	GX-32739/Beta/ext	22,380 ± 800	01/06/2007	MT
Hadrosaur #2	GX-32678/AMS/w	22,990 ± 130	04/04/2007	MT
Hadrosaur #2	UGAMS-01935/AMS/bio	25,670 ± 220	04/10/2007	MT
Hadrosaur #2	UGAMS-01936/AMS/w	25,170 ± 230	04/10/2007	MT
Hadrosaur #2	UGAMS-01937/AMS/col	23,170 ± 170	04/10/2007	MT
Hadrosaur #3	UGAMS-9893/AMS/bio	37,660 ± 160	11/29/2011	CO
Apatosaur	UGAMS-9891/AMS/bio	38,250 ± 160	11/29/2011	CO

You will Notice the Date Ranges (Between 20 and 40 Thousand years old), are Identical to Those from Woolly Mammoths (Ancient Elphants), Saber Tooth Tigers (Ancient Cats), etc...

This is Because All these Giant Animals come from the Same Ecological Time Frame, and were Breathing the same Atmosphere.

In Short, they All Lived Before the Flood.

A FEW FUN EXAMPLES FROM BOB ENYART'S "NOT SO OLD THINGS"

1) Opals Form in "A Few Months" And Don't Need 100,000 Years as previously claimed.

A 2011 peer-reviewed paper in a geology journal from Australia, where almost all the world's opal is found, reported on the: "new timetable for opal formation involving weeks to a few months and not the hundreds of thousands of years envisaged by the conventional weathering model."

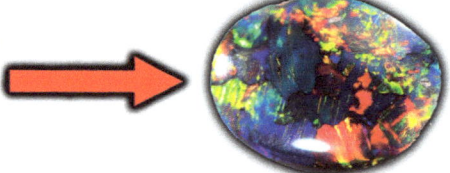

2) Finches Speciate in Two Generations NOT Two Million Years for Darwin's Birds.

Darwin's finches on the Galapagos Islands are said to have diversified into 14 species over a period of two million years. But in 2017, the journal Science reported a newcomer to the Island which within two generations spawned a reproductively isolated new species. This is merely a variation in species type, called Micro-evolution ~ far different from from a Rhino becoming a turtle, a monkey a person, or a T-Rex a bird.

3) Stalactites & Stalagmites form in years NOT millions of years.

A construction worker in 1954 left a lemonade bottle in one of Australia's famous Jenolan Caves. By 2011, it had been naturally transformed into a stalagmite. There are now many, many examples like this of quick growing cave formations globally.

4) Polystrate Trees ~ Trees standing upright through strata.

-Yellowstone's petrified polystrate forest with successive layers of rootless trees demonstrating the rapid deposition of fifty layers of strata.
- A similarly formed polystrate fossil forest in France demonstrating the rapid deposition of a dozen strata.
- In a thousand locations including famously the Fossil Cliffs of Joggins, Nova Scotia, polystrate fossils such as trees span many strata.

5) Nautiloids (Squid) standing on their heads In the Grand Canyon

In the limestone layer averaging seven feet thick that runs the 277 miles of the Grand Canyon contains an average of one nautiloid fossil per square meter. Along with many other dead creatures in this one particular layer ~ about one fifth of these nautiloids were killed and then fossilized standing on their heads, vertically in the strata.

6) Evolution now claims the Ocean is NOT getting saltier.

I am personally adding this one in myself, because Darwin supporters do NOT get a "Free Pass on Reality" just because they managed to put a couple of poorly written papers by Evolution-loving professors up online. They now claim the Ocean is not getting saltier ~ the reason they state that is because if it were getting saltier, then in under a 100 thousand years everything in the oceans would be dead ~ like the Dead sea in Israel.

This single fact would mean the Oceans are less than 100 thousand years old ~ In short, this single arguement would mean evolution never happened <-- for this cause, they have to fight it.

Yes, the Ocean's ARE getting saltier ~ and all the two cent webpages of colorful professors crying, and five dollar university words won't stop the ocean getting saltier.

Rivers carry the salts of the Earth into the Oceans, the salts do not evaporate from there, but build up in the oceans. yes indeed, obviously, everything in the ocean over time would perish.

7) Neither strata nor ice cores are tree rings

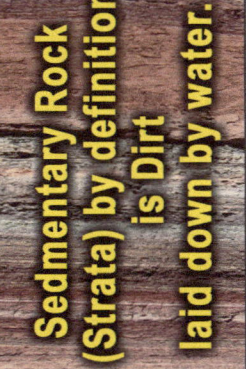

Sedmentary Rock (Strata) by definition is Dirt laid down by water.

World War II Airplanes are Under the Ice in the same areas as ice cores are drilled. The Greenland Society of Atlanta has recently attempted to excavate a 10 foot diameter shaft in the Greenland ice pack to remove two B17 Flying Fortresses and six P38 Lightning fighters trapped under an estimated 300 feet of ice for almost 50 years (Bloomberg, 1989).

This means the ice sheet has been accumulating at an average rate of five feet per year. The Greenland ice sheet averages almost 4000 feet thick. If we were to assume the ice sheet has been accumulating at this rate since its beginning, it would take less than 1000 years for it to form. ~ credit ICR & Answers in Genesis

Dragons
The Death Pose

Strata, as seen in this image, is commonly compared to tree rings.

TO BE VERY CLEAR, STRATA IS DIRT.

It is sorted in layers the same way water sorts rocks, dirt and earth. This process is called liquifaction ~ sorting the sediments from heaviest to lightest.

The Strata Layers are made of Sedimentary Rocks ~ which by very definition are sediments laid down by water.

Within those layers are billions of dead things sorted by ecological systems in mass.

The ancient dragons, now called dinosaurs, are commonly found in the DEATH POSE.

Dinosaurs are commonly found in mass burials in the "Death Pose". This is because they were buried almost immediately, the necks are violently bent upwards, often broken, as they were gasping for breath.

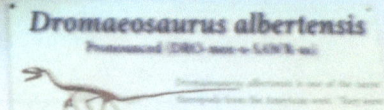

Dromaeosaurus albertensis

ICE CORES

In this image is Dima, one of the most well preserved baby mammoths. Below to the right, is the frozen Berezovka mammoth, the first ever found.

Mammoths are commonly found frozen while standing up.

They have tropical food in their mouths and stomachs ~ this means whatever "froze" them happened nearly instantly. And, the enviroment they lived in went from tropical to ice at a rapid rate.

If water is bursting into the atmosphere from major eruption sites on Earth, it will come down as sheer ice.

Also, if ice cores truly represented millions of years, it's strange how these ancient elephants could stand upward and let millions of years of ice build up around them. Obviously, they would have rotted in months.

Just like the strata ~ it is not just ancient elephants, mammoths, but entire ecological systems frozen in time. And, ice is actually frozen water ~ frozen water that engulfed these creatures in seconds.

The Truth is: Among the Elites of this world, pre-flood artifacts are the most valuable things on Earth.

Now, going a step further, if you find frozen ecological systems on just the edges of the ice ~ what do you think may also be "frozen in time" should one have the funding to go deeper?

Or have they...

Entire Ancient Cities and their Pre-Flood technologies, perhaps?

Scarier Thought: In this nuclear age ~ Do you think there may be others in places of power asking those very Questions?

SOFTWARE DNA OF LIFE

Evolution should have been abandoned when the DNA molecular structure and clear software coding was first identified by Francis Crick and James Watson at the Cavendish Laboratory within the University of Cambridge in 1953.

Since that time, evolutionists began by claiming there was lots of junk coding. This claim has not only been disproven reduntantly over time ~ but as any coder knows, a program does NOT work if it is full of "junk code."

Following the failure of "junk code" evolution arguments, they began trying to compare monkey (typically chimpanzee) DNA to human DNA and attempting to find similarities.

For anyone with a background in coding, these arguments surpass mere foolish, but enter the realm of both desparate and ~ frankly ~ embarrassing.

A single cell of a human, plant or any animal (that we can barely see under our largest microscopes) has more machinery than every automated car factory, and every NASA space shuttle combined ~ and that is just one single cell.

Now, you need the software for that cell ~ the DNA.

Imagine if you had all that machinery but even slightly the wrong software, it would not function.

Accordingly, if I took a copy of Microsoft Windows and a copy of Adobe Photoshop (both light years less sofisticated than the precision coding of one strand of DNA) ~ a laymen or expert could see them as quite similar. They are both written in the same programming languadge. Yet, they can not "evolve" into one another ~ not without serious intelligent help.

The Bible divides things into kinds, just like the illustration to the left.

You can have many variations within the program Windows, just like you can have many variations within the coding for dogs.

You can have bald dogs, hairy dogs, tall dogs, small dogs, etc... within dog coding. But, you do not have turtle shells in "dog code" nor do you have bird wings. The coding has limitation.

Dogs make dogs. Turtles make turtles. People make people.

It really is that simple.

So, the base framework of our 3 dimensional "reality" operates much like a vastly more robust and elegant version of the primitive binary code of our computers.

Binary Code

Reality is a framework of quantum particles.

Within that framework, you find that all biological "Entities" ~ you, plants and animals ~ are made of software coding

DNA Software

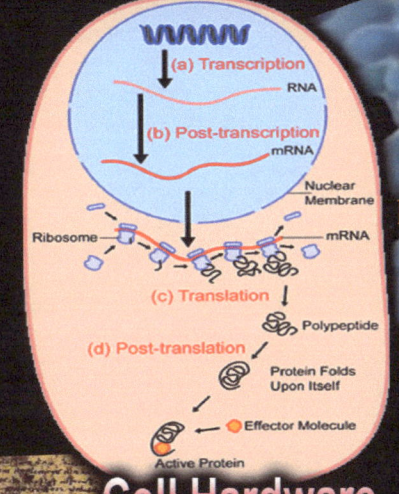

Cell Hardware

Each cell is running software beyond imagination.

Those cells, make organs (like the heart) which if it were NOT perfectly right from the start ~ you would be dead. Those organs work in complete systems, of which ALL the parts have to function from the very start ~ or you would also be dead.

Heart Machinery

Then, you simply need complete "software" body plans ~ organizing every cell, every system, every little piece and part into a complete biological masterpeice ~ from scratch.

And then consciously "plugged-in" as if by WIFI.

This is all a very far cry from a 150 year old Theory by a 22 year old that breeding monkeys makes people. The answers are somewhat larger than that.

Human Body
Full Biological Machine you Operate

Rewind to DNA the Beginning
Mitochondrial Eve

Evolutionists & Universities largely abandoned the research into what they were calling "Mitochondrial Eve" out of terror of what they found. The hope for those grant funded in claimed "Evolution sciences" was to "rewind in time" backwards using DNA mutations to hopefully find monkey like people coming from Africa.

Even the premise of this set of experiments was not terribly good for their cause, and the results worse ~ and the fixes a nightmare. Let me explain why:

First, mutations by their very definition are "Errors in the Coding" collected generation by generation as we are really weakening over time ~ de-evolving (the reverse of the theory).

When discovered, University & Evolution articles had titles such as: "mtDNA mutation rates-no need to panic"

Or, The Journal Science in 1998

"Evolutionists are most concerned about the effect of a faster mutation rate. For example, researchers have calculated that "mitochondrial Eve" --the woman whose mtDNA was ancestral to that in all living people—lived 100,000 to 200,000 years ago in Africa. Using the new clock, she would be a mere 6000 years old."

Furthermore, the mutations (errors) were happening faster then they expected (we are going genetically downhill fast).

Thus, using the actual data, it came to a common "mutation free" mother of us all" 6,000 years ago.

This was unacceptable. So they mixed human data with monkey data ~ largely abandoned the project as to not bring more attention ~ and put forth the large complicated numbers and answers you now see in their newest reports.

Rewind to DNA the Beginning
Y-Chromosomal Adam

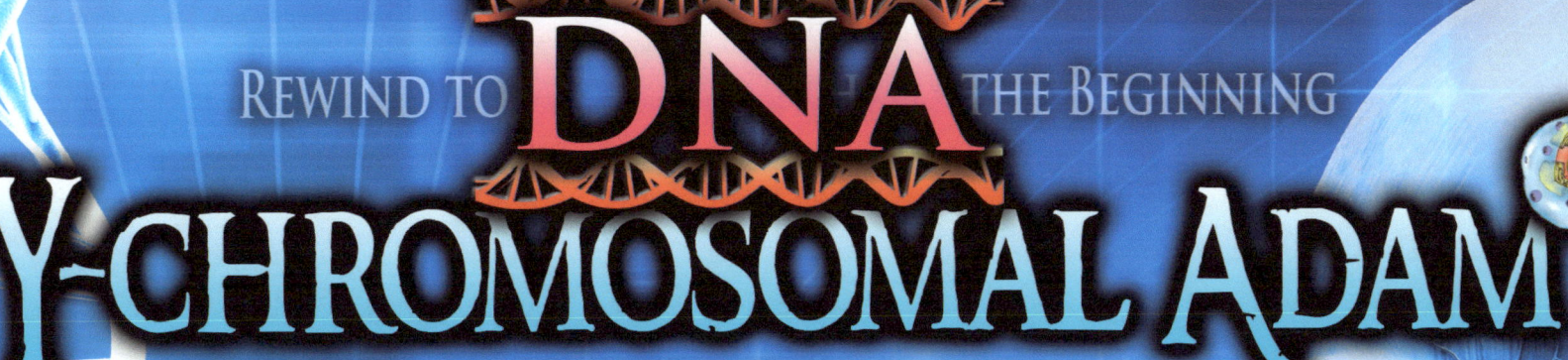

But, the problem is worse than that.

You also have "Genetic Adam," who the actual "Real World Data" put at only a few thousand years old (ballpark of 4,500). Same fix, monkey numbers with "Real Numbers" to get it once again to 200,000 years....

Because that's how real science is done, when you don't get what you like; make stuff up and use BIG words no-one understands.

If one were to guess, the reason Genetic Eve comes to 6,000 is because you actually are tracing back to the first woman (or close). The Genetic Adam is showing you the "Genetic Bottleneck" at the Flood through the Male Gene.

In Layman's Terms, no matter what "Age" you get: You are Rewinding to the Perfect State of mankind by sheer virtue of the test itself.

Further, you are also finding that ALL the people alive today came from a single woman in that "Perfect Genetic State" living roughly 6,000 years ago by the "Real World Data."

Chapter Six

6

MAN, ANGELS & DEVILS

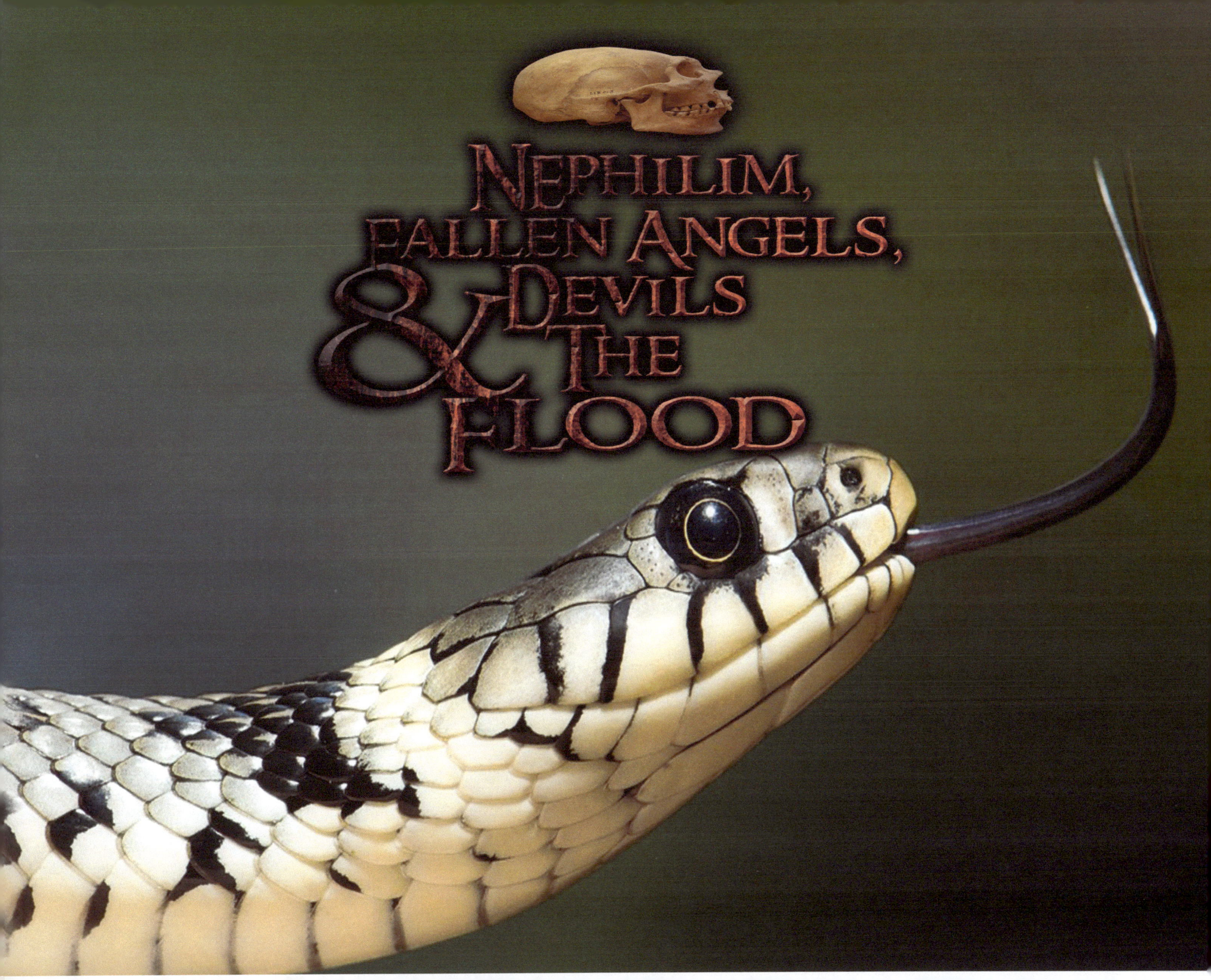

The SuperNatural

Your Ancient Biblical pages are telling you that you are in a place that by any Natural cause ~ would NOT exist.

The Word superNatural merely means, above the Natural ~ above what you can Truly understand. This place is the product of a Larger place.

It is a Created place.

It was Created for Man.

Further, that Eternity ~ the Place from which this place Comes from ~ is teeming with Life.

There are indeed Angels and Devils.

And, All these seemingly Magical Things, are as close as the Air between your fingers.

Like the Two Trees in the Garden, God says: Choose this Day whom you serve.

It is Not the the fear of Devils, but the fear of God which is the beginning of True Wisdom.

ANGELS

The first use of the word "Angel" (in this case Cheribum) in the Torah (Bible) is in Genesis 3:24 ~ Three is the Number of Departments of God, and Twenty-Four is the number of High Authority, Revelation 4:4 declares, "Surrounding the throne were twenty-four other thrones, and seated on them were twenty-four elders."

The "Law of First Mention" is a principle that the First Time a word is used in the Bible, it has special importance ~ just as the Root of Something is where it begins.

"21 Unto Adam also and to his wife did the Lord God make coats of skins, and clothed them.

Notes: This was the first sacrifice ~ for the covering of Adam & Eve's sin, something innocent would have to die.

22 And the Lord God said, Behold, the man is become as one of us, to know good and evil: and now, lest he put forth his hand, and take also of the tree of life, and eat, and live for ever:

23 Therefore the Lord God sent him forth from the garden of Eden, to till the ground from whence he was taken.

24 So he drove out the man; and he placed at the east of the garden of Eden Cherubims, and a flaming sword (A Sword represents the "Word" or "Truth") which turned slung from side to side, to keep the way of the tree of life."

The Flaming Sword represents Jesus: "I am the Way, the Truth and the Life ~ No Man Cometh before the Father except by me." ~ John 14:6

The first time an Angel is mentioned by name is Gabriel in the Book of Daniel to give Daniel the Math and Date of the Messiah.

Daniel wrote his book during the time of Babylonian Captivity for Israel. A time that lasted exactly 70 years.

Daniel 9:25

24 Seventy weeks are decreed for your people ....25 Know and understand this: From the time the decree goes forth to restore and rebuild Jerusalem, until the Messiah, the King comes, there will be seven weeks (These are "weeks of years" as defined by the text) and sixty-two weeks (making a total of 69 to Crucifixion).

26 Then after this, the Messiah will be cut off (Karat), publicly executed.

Trey's Notes: The Sixty Nine (69) "Weeks of Years" leads to the exact date Jesus Christ rode into Jerusalem on the Donkey.

The Angel Gabriel gave Daniel the Math for this over 500 years beforehand.

The last week, the last seven year period, is the most covered period in your entire Bible....

It is the final seven years of Revelation.

Many times in Scripture the people wanted to declare Jesus out as King.. Yet, the text will say he vanished into the crowd, or otherwise got out of the situation.

That is until one particular day, the day Daniel gave the math for.

When Jesus told the Diciples, go over the hills and get me the Donkey... And they asked, "Master, how do you know these things?"

Indeed, I tell you, that Donkey was prepared before these worlds were formed.

Artaxerxes Longimanus Decree to Rebuild Jerusalem
March 14, 445 B.C.

Jesus Triumphal Entry
April 6, 32 A.D.

Exactly 17,880 Days
69 x 7 x 360 Ancient Calendar Days

Enoch's Calendar has 360 days, and 4 days of Rememberance for God. A Perfect: 364

Drone Footage by Trey Smith
City of David, Israel
Where Jesus Rode in on Donkey

Genesis 5:24
And Enoch walked with God, and Enoch was not, for God took him.

Jesus Christ

In my Father's house are many mansions (John 14:2)

Blessed are the meek, for they shall inherit the earth. (Mat 5:5)

Shall inherit everlasting life (Mat. 19:29)

The water that I shall give him shall be in him a well of water springing up into everlasting life. (John 4:14)

Enoch

In that day shall the Elect One sit upon a throne of glory, and shall choose their conditions and countless habitations. (Enoch 45:3)

The elect shall possess light, joy and peace, and they shall inherit the earth. (Enoch 5:7)

Those who will inherit eternal life (Enoch 40:9)

All the thirsty drank, and were filled with wisdom, having their habitation with the righteous, the elect, and the holy. (Enoch 48:1)

Jesus is often quoting scripture, seeming to also include Enoch.

Enoch was the 7th from Adam. Great Grandfather of Noah.

Genesis 5:24

And Enoch walked with God, and ENOCH was Not, for God Took Him.

The Symbol of the "Chet" is the 8th Symbol of Ancient Hebrew. The first part of the "Chet" (the "C") is silent until the end. Just as the first letter of Hebrew (the Aleph) is silent, yet starts everything.

Jesus was Raised from the Dead in 3 Days, on the "8th" Day, of the Week ~ Sunday. That is why Christians today worship on Sunday.

Chet

8

Drone Footage by Trey Smith over Mount of Ascension, Jerusalem, at Night. This shot was taken on Israel's Prophetic 70th Anniversary.

The Eight turned Sideways makes Infinity. Just as the "Chet" is the "New Beginning" Infinity.

80

PRISON OF JESUS

This is believed to be the prison under the Old City of Jerusalem where Jesus was held before Cruxifiction.

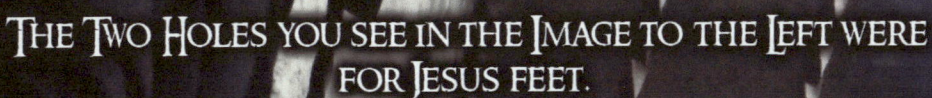

CHET

The two holes you see in the image to the left were for Jesus feet.

He was literally chained underground to a giant stone symbol for new beginnings, or infinity.

81

This is the Mouth of Pan's Cave ~ at the base of Mount Hermon

It is also the Mount of Transfiguration where Jesus changed in form before the Disciples.

It was a Message to Darkness.

Mount Hermon

"By the order of the Most High and Holy God, those who swear an oath proceed from here."

The "god" is probably Baal-Hermon.

~Translation by Derek Gilbert

An Ancient Stela was Discovered atop Mt. Hermon which honored the Preflood Fall of the Angels & Azazel (the Goat).

Matthew 17 (Seven and One is 8)

After six days Jesus took with him Peter, James and John the brother of James, and led them up a high mountain by themselves. 2 There he was transfigured before them. His face shone like the sun, and his clothes became as white as the light. 3 Just then there appeared before them Moses and Elijah, talking with Jesus.

4 Peter said to Jesus, "Lord, it is good for us to be here. If you wish, I will put up three shelters—one for you, one for Moses and one for Elijah."

5 While he was still speaking, a bright cloud covered them, and a voice from the cloud said, "This is my Son, whom I love; with him I am well pleased. Listen to him!"

6 When the disciples heard this, they fell facedown to the ground, terrified. 7 But Jesus came and touched them. "Get up," he said. "And FEAR NOT."

8 When they looked up, they saw no one except Jesus.

This is Also the Exact Spot where Jesus Pointed at Peter and said:

"Get Behind Me Satan!"

Greek God Pan

83

GENESIS 6

6 When man began to increase in number on the earth and daughters were born to them, 2 the sons of God (Bene-Ha Elohim ~ Angels, or in this context, Fallen Angels) saw that the daughters of men were beautiful, and they came down and took wives of any of them they chose.

3 Then the Lord said, "My Spirit will not contend with man forever, for they are mortal; their days will be a hundred and twenty years."

4 The Nephilim were on the earth in those days—and also afterward—when the sons of God went to the daughters of men and had children by them. They were the heroes (legends) of old, men of renown.

5 The Lord saw how great the wickedness of the man had become on the earth, and that every inclination of the thoughts of the human heart was only evil all the time.

6 It grieved the Lord that He had made man, and his heart was deeply troubled.

8 But Noah found favor in the eyes of the Lord.

ENOCH 6

1. And it came to pass when the children of men had multiplied that in those days were born unto them beautiful and comely daughters. 2. And the angels, the children of the heaven, saw and lusted after them, and said to one another: 'Come, let us choose us wives from among the children of men and beget us children.'

3. And Semjâzâ, (also with next in command Azâzêl) was their leader....

6. And they were in all two hundred; who descended in the days of Jared on the summit of Mount Hermon.

7. And these are the names of their leaders: Sêmiazâz, their leader Arâkiba, Râmêêl, Kôkabiêl, Tâmiêl, Râmiêl, Dânêl, Ezêqêêl, Barâqijâl, Asâêl, Armârôs, Batârêl, Anânêl, Zaqiêl, Samsâpêêl, Satarêl, Tûrêl, Jômjâêl, Sariêl.

8. These are their chiefs of tens.

8

There are two new beginnings on these pages. One new beginning for man, and one new beginning for Darkness.

The Fallen Angels were the Pagan World's gods.

Lilith

Lilith is a figure in Jewish mythology & Babylonian Talmud ~ She is a sexual demon of the night, who steals babies in the darkness.

Lilith is sometimes claimed in these Mythologies as Adam's first wife, before Eve. There is No support for this in the Biblical Text.

However, Enoch seems to give some clarity to the character of Lilith.

> Enoch 19:1. And Uriel (The Angel that gave Enoch the Calendar) said to me: 'Here shall stand the angels who have connected themselves with women, and their spirits assuming many different forms are defiling mankind and shall lead them astray into sacrificing to demons as gods, here shall they stand, till the ay of the great judgement in which they shall be judged till they are made an end of. 2. And the women also of the angels who went astray shall become sirens.' 3. And I, Enoch, alone saw the vision, the ends of all things: and no man shall see as I have seen."

Lilith is translated as "night creatures", "night monster", "night hag", or "screech owl" ~ literally a female Night Demon "Siren" that enters by seduction, then controls.

Occult traditions coming from Babylon twisted this to be Adam's first wife.

However, we can see that becoming a "Lilith" (Siren) is the very Curse lasting to the day of judgment put on the Women who voluntarily bound themselves to Fallen Angels before the Flood.

Inanna
The Ancient Madonna of Earth, hailing the One Ruler of Earth ~ first AntiChrist, Nimrod ~ whilst holding captive the Lion.

Ishtar
Or Inanna "Queen of Heaven" the patron goddess of the Eanna temple at the city of Uruk, Defied Wife of Nimrod ~ depicted here as a Siren.

ENOCH Chapter 69

Cave & Child Sacrifice Site At Base of Mt. Hermon

3. And these are the chiefs of their angels and their names, and their chief ones over hundreds and over fifties and over tens.

4. The name of the first Jeqon: that is, the one who led astray [all] the sons of God (Fallen Angels), and brought them down to the earth, and led them astray through the daughters of men. 5. And the second was named Asbeel: he imparted to the holy sons of God evil counsel, and led them astray so that they defiled their bodies with the daughters of men. 6. And the third was named Gadreel: he it is who showed the children of men all the blows of death, and he led astray Eve, and showed the weapons of death to the sons of men.

12. And the fifth was named Kasdeja: this is he who showed the children of men all the wicked smitings of spirits and demons, and the smitings of the embryo in the womb (Abortion), that it may pass away, and [the smitings of the soul] the bites of the serpent, and the smitings which befall through the noontide heat, the son of the serpent named Tabâêt.

Chapter 15 Nephilim and Demons

8. And now, the giants, who are produced from the spirits and flesh, shall be called evil spirits upon the earth, and on the earth shall be their dwelling. 9. Evil spirits have proceeded from their bodies; because they are born from men, and from the Holy Watchers is their beginning and primal origin; they shall be evil spirits on earth, and evil spirits shall they be called, on the earth shall be their dwelling.

11. And the spirits of the giants (Nephilim) afflict, oppress, destroy, attack, do battle, and work destruction on the earth, and cause trouble: they take no food, but nevertheless hunger and thirst, and cause offences.

And these spirits shall rise up against the children of men and against the women, because they have proceeded from them.....

Just as in The Preflood World, all the way to the Ancient Sacrifice Altars for Children from the base of Mount Hermon, to the Towering Temples in South American Jungles following the Flood...

There seems to be a Serious Interest in the Sacrifice of Children, even in the Womb.

In the Ancient World, Women were invited to The Most Dazzling of Well Funded Temples to Kill Their Babies...

Ken and Jo Scott have fought Abortion for Decades. Ken used to be one of the Most Successful Real Estate Moguls in Denver, Colorado. He gave That up to help Women, and the Children that They were minutes from Aborting.

They have been called Scum and Sleeze for Saving Babies Lives over the Years by Major Medias. They have also fought many False Felonies (also for saving babies), and Endless Civil Actions against themselves and their Families.

They Would say: "If it saved One Baby's Life, It was Worth it." They have saved Many Hundreds....

87

Inside Pan's Cave
at Base of Hermon

Ancient Altar in Pan's Cave

Strangely Giant Pile of Bird / Bat Dung on Altar

Inside Pan's Cave, where Jesus said: "Get behind me Satan!"

There is an unnaturally giant pile of dung on the altar for child sacrifice.

Dung on Altar

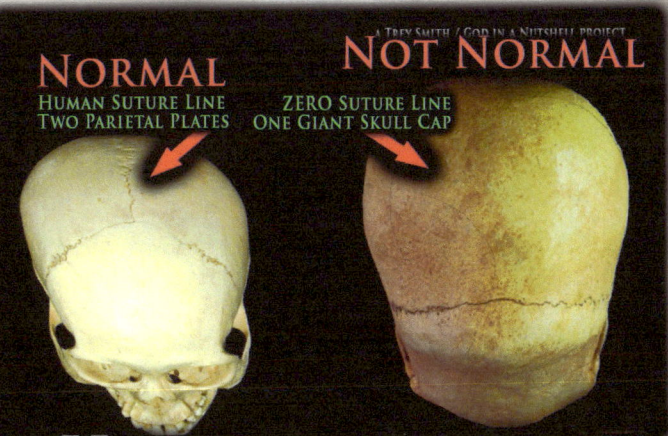

HUMAN NEPHILIM?

Elongated Skulls are a Global Phenomenon; but nowhere are they as prevalent as in South America.

Some of this is done by head-binding. But, other skulls are clearly naturally "Elongated." Additionally, some of the more dramatic "Elongated Skulls" have a different skull structure then modern, or even ancient humans (as Seen Above).

In truth, no-one knows exactly what these skulls are? They could be called "Nephilim" for lack of a better term. They come well after the flood & they're Weird.

What we do know is Child Sacrifice is VERY WELL documented for these cultures.

And the Strange Skulls often appear to be Royalty at major Occult Ritual and sacrifice Sites.

Quetzalcoatl
~ The Feathered Serpent ~

This Serpent (a "Wisdom Serpent") was often seen Occult Trance states and worshipped as a god by the Mayans, Incas, Aztecs, and other MesoAmericans.

Quetzalcoatl the Serpent is the Aztec god of wind, and Prince of the air.

Does this sound familiar to a certain Snake in Genesis?

MACHU PICCHU

PHOTO: MARTIN ST-AMANT - WIKIPEDIA - CC-BY-SA3.0

Henry Shaffer

is the President of Radio Station 99.9 FM in New Ellenton, South Carolina. He also is a well recognized Deliverance Minister ~ what the Catholic Church would call "Exorcism."

In the image above he has set up a chair for a Deliverance sessions. Some of these can be "Demonically Intense."

Below, fluids are coming from a woman's mouth as she convulses during Shaffer's Deliverance and teachings in the Mayan jungle.

Don Jeffrey

is seen here holding a South American "Elongated Skull" and comparing it to a human skull.

Don is a Retired Police Detective, and was also a part of the Famous "Cold Case Posse."

He takes interest in dramatic Demonic Possesion and Deliverance cases, often also those claiming serious beliefs that aliens arf abuducting and terrorizing them.

Black Magician Eliphas Levi is Pictured here using a "Grimoire" (Book of Ritual Magick).

He has opened a Portal to the Dark World to Summon an Ancient Wisdom Demon called a "Yoda."

Image Source: "An encyclopedic Outline of Masonic, Hermetic, Quabbalist and Rosicrucian Sumbolical Philosophy."

The gray alien looking creature called "Lam" and its depiction was heavily sworn by Crowley to be what the "Dimensional Entity" looked like when it came through what he called "Magickal Portals."

In both the Bible and Enoch, demons and angels are in a dimension side-by-side with the one you are in; like hitting the "show code" key on reality.

In fact, that "Spiritual World" of God, angels and devils is more "real" than this world. It is the place where this place comes from. ~ Trey Smith

Aleister Crowley

Today, even as you sit to read this page, Aleister Crowley knows the Truth. And, his life pursuing the love of these devils cost him everything. It cost him eternity and all its wonders.

If only he knew what he knows now.

Choose this day whom you serve?

Lam ~ "The Alien Intelligence," as Crowley described it ~ was somehow also in connection with another entity called: Aiwass.

"Behold! it is revealed by Aiwass the minister of Hoor-paar-kraat."

"Hoor-paar-kraat" means "Horus the Child."

God gives stiff instructions not to deal, or communicate with these entities.... even the Devil himself appears as an angel of light.

"Lam" from Crowley's "Book of the Law"

"My name is called Aiwass," Crowley writes, "in the Book of the Law did I write the secrets of truth (Dictated by Aiwass) that are like unto a Star and a Snake and a Sword."

Aiwass was described by Crowley as an Assyrian / Sumerian looking ancient king who had him write the Book of the Law which was to be a precursor to an "Aeon of Horus." This claimed Sumerian / Assyrian king appeared to Crowley over three days: April 8, 9, and 10 in 1904.

This Magical Assyrian King and his "Alien / Demon" messenger (Lam) stepping through "Portals" in our reality have strinking similarities to Nimrod's wicked son, Mardon, who claimed to be birthed by his true father: the Enki ~ stepping from a portal to the Abyss (where Enki rules with his wisdom serpents).

Enki, seen beneath, is stepping through a portal with crow & witches hat (false tree of life) during the time of Nimrod.

"Enki"

THE WAY

Lam is the Tibetan word for Way or Path, and Lama is He who Goeth, the specific title of the Gods of Egypt, the Treader of the Path, in Buddhistic phraseology. Its numerical value is 71, the number of this book.

ENOCH
Chapter 46:1-2 — PREFLOOD

There I beheld the Ancient of Days whose head was like white wool, and with him another, whose countenance resembled that of a man. His countenance was full of grace, like that of one of the holy angels.

Then I inquired of one of the angels, who went with me, and who showed me these secret things, concerning this Son of man; who he was; whence he was; and why he accompanied the Ancient of Days.

He answered and said to me, This is the Son of man, to whom all righteousness belongs; with whom righteousness has dwelt; and who will reveal all the treasures of that which is concealed: for the Lord of Spirits has chosen him; and his portion has surpassed all before the Lord of Spirits in everlasting uprightness."

DANIEL
Chapter 7 — OLD TESTAMENT

9 "As I looked,

"Thrones were set in place,
and the Ancient of Days took his seat.
His clothing was as white as snow;
the hair of his head was white like wool.
His throne was flaming with fire,
and its wheels were all ablaze.
10 A river of fire was flowing,
coming out from before him.
Thousands upon thousands attended him;
ten thousand times ten thousand stood before him.
The court was seated,
and the books were opened.

ENOCH
Chapter 14 : 8-9 — Preflood

8. And the vision was shown to me thus: Behold, in the vision clouds invited me and a mist summoned me, and the course of the stars and the lightnings sped and hastened me, and the winds in the vision caused me to fly and lifted me upward, and bore me into heaven. 9. And I went in till I drew nigh to a wall which is built of crystals and surrounded by tongues of fire: and it began to affright me. And I went into the tongues of fire and drew nigh to a large house which was built of crystals: and the walls of the house were like a tesselated floor (made) of crystals, and its groundwork was of crystal.

REVELATION
Chapter 4 — New Testament

After this I looked, and there before me was a door standing open in heaven. And the voice I had first heard speaking to me like a trumpet said, "Come up here, and I will show you what must take place after this." 2 At once I was in the Spirit, and there before me was a throne in heaven with someone sitting on it. 3 And the one who sat there had the appearance of jasper and ruby. A rainbow that shone like an emerald encircled the throne. 4 Surrounding the throne were twenty-four other thrones, and seated on them were twenty-four elders. They were dressed in white and had crowns of gold on their heads. 6 Also in front of the throne there was what looked like a sea of glass, clear as crystal.

ENOCH Chapter 14 (and 15)

18. And I looked and saw a lofty throne: its appearance was as crystal, and the wheels thereof as the shining sun, and there was the vision of cherubim. 19. And from underneath the throne came streams of flaming fire so that I could not look thereon. 20. And the Great Glory sat thereon, and His raiment shone more brightly than the sun and was whiter than any snow.

24. And until then I had been prostrate on my face, trembling: and the Lord called me with His own mouth, (Chapter 15) and said to me: 'Fear not, Enoch, thou righteous man and scribe of righteousness 2. And go, say to the Watchers of heaven (Fallen Angels), who have sent thee to intercede for them: "You should intercede" for men, and not men for you."

ENOCH
Chapter 47 — Preflood

1 In that day the prayer of the holy and the righteous, and the blood of the righteous, shall ascend from the earth into the presence of the Lord of spirits.

3 At that time I beheld the Ancient of days, while he sat upon the throne of his glory, while the book of the living was opened before Him, and while all the powers which were above the heavens stood around.

DANIEL
Chapter 7 — Old Testament

10 And the books were opened (same book Moses saw on the Mountain).

11 Then I continued to watch because of the boastful words the horn (anti-christ) was speaking. I kept looking until the beast was slain and its body destroyed and thrown into the blazing fire.

13 (with the disciples Jesus would be number 13, the chaos number) "In my vision at night I looked, and there before me was one like a son of man, coming with the clouds of heaven. He approached the Ancient of Days and was led into his presence. 14 He was given authority, glory and sovereign power; all nations and peoples of every language worshiped him.

ENOCH
~Chapter 48~

1 In that place I beheld a fountain of righteousness, which never failed, encircled by many springs of wisdom. Of these all the thirsty drank.

2 In that hour was this Son of man named before the Lord of spirits, and his name in the presence of the Ancient of days.

3 Yea, before the sun and the signs were created, before the stars of heaven were made, his name was named in the presence of the Lord of spirits. He shall be a staff for the righteous and the holy to lean upon, that they might not fall; and he shall be the light of all nations.

God, Aliens & Preflood Devils

All alive and well ~ You are in a flesh space suit wondering in in a Spiritual battleground.

The "mare" in the Word "Nightmare" comes from the Old Norse incubus: the "Mara" ~ attacking at night. The "MAra Demon" over time has for some been an old hag (Siren), cloaked druids for others, and now Morphing for many today into Evil Aliens standing around the bed.

The Incubus & Female succubus have been documented to the Dawn of written history in a wealth of forms ~ now today called in Psychology, "sleep paralysis" (the Demon on the Chest)."

It is estimated that more than 50% of people have experienced "sleep paralysis demons," and an even higher number believing they have had a supernatural experience they normally don't talk about. Probability states, you reading this page are in that group.

Major medical facilities, such as Johns Hopkins, are now doing research on those who frequentlty take drugs such as DMT to meet with "DMT Aliens." These creatures & entities are often described as aliens, demons, angels & machine elves with consistent descriptions that are eerie. In ancient witchcraft, the easiest way to communicate with devils was always "pharmakia (drugs)" ~ also translated as: witchcraft.

It was (and is to this very day by occultists) believed the world of devils & spirits is a parallel realm, and the drugs open the "mind's eye" to see the edges of what is otherwise invisible. If that be the case, it means the devils and things "attacking" are still there even when the drugs wear off.

1952 Washington, D.C. UFO incident

"Never before or after did Project Blue Book and the Air Force undergo such a tidal wave of (UFO) reports."

On a grander scale, things are recorded in the skies regularly in this age of cells phones. The "UFO phenomenon" appears localized to earth, if something were coming from other planets ~ why can no-one sense the traffic? Additionally, if something just "appears" and "disappears" the Question really becomes ~ Where is it when you don't see it?

Famous researchers such Dr. Jacques Vallée and Dr. J. Allen Hynek put forth in abundance their professional opinions that not only is the phenomenon "real;" but further, that the aliens of this modern age and the demons of the past are probably identical.

In his early career, Dr. Carl Smith worked at some of the most Top Secret Government Research Facilities on Earth ~ I wish i was allowed to delve further into that even as I type this page.

What I can tell you is that growing up, he impressed upon me very greatly that evolution never happened, and that "No-one who was really anyone" believed in it. He was a professor of advanced mathmatics in his later life (whilst doing AI for Shell Oil company). He is still alive & well today, and still believes one of God's languages is Math, as God created Numbers ~ After all, God wrote the "Book of Numbers."

On an interesting note I can discuss, he developed some of the security software where the Alien Bodies were alledgedly taken following Area 51: Wright Patterson, in Ohio.

He was living in Houston, Texas and visiting companies that had made job offers to him. He said that he didn't really like any of them; but knew he had to pick one....

In the midst of the Towering Buildings of Downtown Houston, while driving down the road, he says a Voice came out of thin air. This is ONE of THREE times in his life he says this happened (another occasion the voice said: "You're not going to die today" and a few other things during a heart attack).

The Voice said: "Your job is waiting for you in that building RIGHT THERE."

Dr. Carl Smith near his home in Colorado

Father of Trey Smith

He flipped an illegal u-turn in traffic. Then, walking inside the Giant Ivory Tower Building, he didn't even know what the company was. But, there was a large Marble Stone Front Desk with a Secretary.

Approaching the Lady, he said, "My name is Carl Smith. I recently heard you may be looking for some good people."

He failed to mention to her that he had heard this from a voice that came out of thin air while driving down the road outside by himself just five minutes earlier.

The lady asked, "Sir, do you have an appointment?"

"No..... I just felt strongly I should stop in."

"Well," she continued, "Let me just see if there is anyone that could take time to speak with you."

A little while later she emerged and said, Someone will see you now."
He was then invited into an office by a man who came down from the elevator.

He says he spent several hours with this man.

PASSING BY THESE THREE BUILDINGS

"But, in the end," the man said, "Unfortunately, I don't think we're hiring anyone right now."

"However," he rose to his feet from the desk, "that's ok, because I like you. So, we'll just create a job for you here. I have the Power to do that."

 "When can you start?"

That man was one of the Vice Presidents of Shell Oil Company, where Carl Smith would retire from 20 years later.

He spent his career working on Top Level "Special Projects."

Dr. Carl Smith also became Shell Oil Company's University Recuiter, as well their "Artificial Intelligence Guy" in the 1980's.

His career was spent directly under the presidents and Vice Presidents of Shell Oil and their Research & Development projects.

This "Voice" says to me

Dr. Carl Smith telling the Story

Drone Footage
by Trey Smith
Garden of the Gods
Colorado

Legends of the Flood

There are more than 277 flood accounts from all around the globe.

Rocks that jet straight upwards DO NOT form slowly over time. In fact, your mountain ranges are in the center of continents, and "crumpling" mountain ranges along coastlines. Rocks and Mountains erode downwards. It takes a MAJOR Global Cataclysm to get these formations.

Matthew 24

37 But as the days of Noah were, so also shall the coming of the Son of man be.

Chapter Seven

The Noah Project

Flood Legends

Egypt

The preflood people were wicked. Atum says he will destroy all he made and return the earth to the Primordial Water. Atum then claims he will transform back into his original form of the serpent, with Osiris.

Babylonian

The version the world rulers of today really like most.

The Preflood World had become overpopulated, thus the "gods" sent a global flood.

The "gods" had already tried plague and disease to no avail.

Enki had Atrahasis (Noah) build an ark. After the flood, Enki shows Atrahasis birth control and how to cause still born (dead) babies. This way only "desirables" are born in the future.

Garden of the Gods

Colorado

Garden of the Gods is located right on the edge of the Rocky Mountains, which are in the center of the United States.

These mammoth red stones jet straight upward from the earth as a grand testimony to the hours the fountains of the great deep burst open.

Your major mountain ranges, like the Rocky Mountains, were formed by the enourmous pressures of the Great Flood.

GLOBAL FLOOD
Hydroplate Theory — by Dr. Walt Brown

Walt Brown received a Ph.D. in mechanical engineering at MIT.

Brown is a retired Air Force full colonel, West Point graduate, and former Army Ranger and paratrooper.

He was the Director of Benét Laboratorie and tenured professor at the U.S. Air Force Academy.

Also the Chief of Science and Technology Studies at the Air War College.

He also Developed Hydroplate Theory- which explains Most Every Major Geological Feature of the Earth by the Marine Catastrophy of the Global Flood.

Underneath your Oceans, you find the Mid-Ocean Ridge. This is a fracture encircling the entire Globe. Infact, there is still Water at unbelieveably Hot Temperatures spirting from Trillions of Vents in that Ridge Even Today.

The World before the Flood had Giant Cavernous Pockets of water under the Earth. These Pockets played a Clear Role in facilitating the Giant Plants, and Enormous Ecological Systems, and thereby the Giant "Garden of Eden Style Wildlife" that you see in the Fossil Record Today.

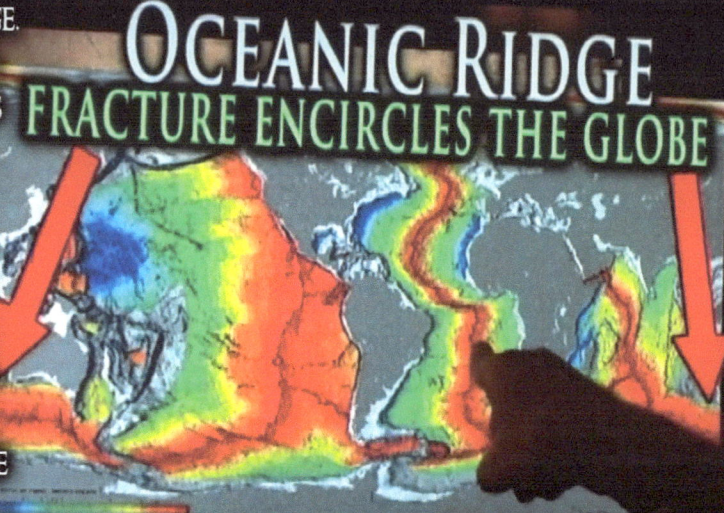

One Hairline Fracture Puncturing One of these Ocean Size Underground Pockets, And the Pressure Would be so intense the Waters of the Great Deeps would Burst forth. This Crack would follow the Path of Least Resistance and encircle the Entire Globe in Merely Minutes. The Heat of the Volcanic Water would Vaporize anything Near it. The Pressure Literally Spraying Water and Rocks as high as Space.

This Water would Rain like an Ocean of Frozen Sludge freezing Entire Ecological Systems Nearly Instantly on some parts of the Planet.

Your Current Seven Continents would be Pushed Upwards between the Fracture Zones (your Modern Oceans). The Mountain Ranges in the Center of those Continents Would Buckle upwards under the intense Pressure Squeezing Inward as the Water Burst forth.

NÜWA

IN THE CHINESE FLOOD ACCOUNT:

LIKE ENDLESS BOILING WATER, THE FLOOD IS POURING FORTH DESTRUCTION. BOUNDLESS AND OVERWHELMING, IT OVERTOPS HILLS AND MOUNTAINS. RISING AND EVER RISING, IT THREATENS THE VERY HEAVENS. HOW THE PEOPLE MUST BE GROANING AND SUFFERING!

—EMPEROR YAO, IN "THE BOOK OF HISTORY," DESCRIBING THE FLOOD

THE PERSON OF "NÜWA" HAS BECOME A GOD IN CHINESE OVER TIME, SOMETIMES BOTH MALE OR FEMALE. THIS IS FOLLOWING GOD MAKING COPIES OF HIM, OR HERSELF, FROM THE MUD OF THE GROUND IN ORDER TO HAVE COMPANIONSHIP.

THE SURVIVORS OF THE CHINESE GREAT FLOOD ARE ~ THE "THREE SOVEREIGNS" NAMED AS NÜ WA, FU XI, AND SHEN NONG SHI ~ AND THE "FIVE EMPERORS."

$3 + 5 = 8$

ALSO, THE VERY WORD FOR "BOAT" IN CHINESE IS THE SYMBOL FOR 8 PEOPLE OR MOUTHS.

IN CHINA, THE 11:11 PHENOMENON IS SO COMMON, IT HAS BECOME A NATIONAL HOLIDAY ON 11/11 EVERY YEAR.

ALSO, THE CHINESE BELIEVE 666 TO BE A VERY LUCKY NUMBER.

GLOBAL FLOOD
The Death of their World is Lighting Yours

It is said the Oil Deposits are Dead Dinosaurs. This has been a fun Theme for some Gas Companies over the Years....

The Truth is Far Larger than that though.... There are Millions and Millions of Cars on the Roads Each and Every Day.

When You are Looking at Oil Deposits you are Looking at Entire Ecological Systems... Giant Forests and Everything in them Swallowed by Earth and Stone... Rolled Up Biological Material Compressed into Pockets of Enormous Size by Massive Pressure under the Ground.

Beneath is called the "Death Pose." It is a Common Way Dinos are found. You can see the Animal is trapped Suddenly and Gasping for breath.

Companies, such as Shell Oil, have Known for Decades that Oil Can be Formed in Minutes by Massive Heat and Pressure.

So, In a Very Real Way, the Death of their World.... Is Lighting Yours.

104

Dromaeosaurus albertensis

JASHER 6

1 At that time, after the death of Methuselah, the Lord said to Noah, Go thou with thy household into the ark; behold I will gather to thee all the animals of the earth, the beasts of the field and the fowls of the air, and they shall all come and surround the ark.

17 And the sons of men assembled together, about seven hundred thousand men and women, and they came unto Noah to the ark. 18 And they called to Noah, saying, Open for us that we may come to thee in the ark--and wherefore shall we die?

20 Is not this the thing that I spoke to you of one hundred and twenty years back, and you would not hearken to the voice of the Lord. 23 But now you come and tell me this on account of the troubles of your souls ~ Then they rushed the boat, yet the animals which surrounded kicked outwards, scattering them.

In that moment, the Waters came inward. 29 And great anxiety seized all the living creatures that were in the ark, and the ark was like to be broken.

Every Creature cried out in its own Tongue!

The Boat Spiralled Upwards,

31 And Noah, gripping for life, cried unto the Lord: on account of this, and he said, "Oh Lord, Remember us. Remember me, Your Servant!...... And deliver us!"

32 And the Lord remembered Noah.

33 And at that moment, the Boat rested peacefully atop the Waters.

WORLD POPULATION

You have Seven Ages of Empires. These Are: The Sumerian/Assyrians, The Egyptians, The Babylonians, The Persians, The Greeks, The Romans...

And Then Many would Call the Hours you Live in Now: Rome Phase II

You have Very Good Records Covering The Slow Conquering of The Entire World.

These Records Begin in the Fertile Cresent, Sumeria/Assyria...

Or, More Specifically, They Begin At the Very Spot Where the "Boat that Saved Mankind" Is said to have Landed.

Population Growth happens much more Rapidly Then Many Realize. Yet, The Math for it is Quite Simple. At Current Rates, the World Population....

👩🧑 → 2% → 6 Billion in 1,100 Years

Doubles about Every 40 years. Starting with Two People on the Planet it Only Takes about 32 "Doublings" to Reach Over 8 Billion.

Now, you have to Take into Account Wars, Famines, Increases in Food Production Abilities.... But a Modest Time Frame to Reach our Current World Population Actually just about Matches Perfectly our Empires and Written Records...

Starting with Eight People you Reach 6 Billion in about 1,100 Years. This Does Not Take into Account Wars, Famines & Natural Disasters.

Again, We Have Full Written Records Going All The Way Back To The First Settlements After The Flood In Sumeria.

To Put This in Greater Perspective, If Mankind Had Been Here 50,000 Years You Should Have:

10,000,000,000,000,000,000,000,000,000,000, 000,000,000,000,000,000,000,000,000,000, 000,000,000,000,000,000,000,000,000,000, 000,000

People on the Planet.... This Also Brings up the Question: Where Are All The Bodies?

NOAH 3500-3000
SUMERIA/ASSYRIA
EGYPT DYNASTY 0 2800BC

The Boat of Noah
Can All the Animals Fit?

Just like populations of people are exponential; populations of animals can be even much more exponential. Greater still, animals "speciate" ~ which is traceable by the way.

By speciate, this means one set of ancient "dogs" makes many later genetic breeds of dogs. One set of cats, many breeds of cats.... etc... etc... etc...

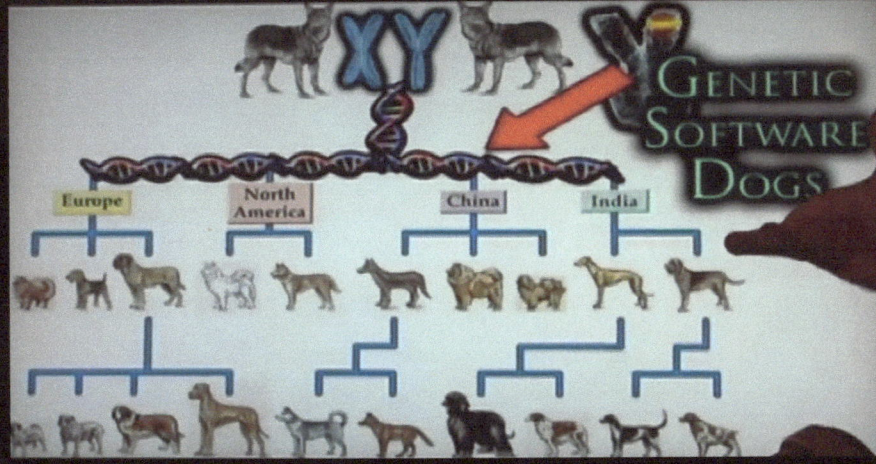

And as we see with humans, the genetics are stronger the further back in time that you go.

In the Book of Jasher, not only is Noah taking the very youngest (smallest & healthiest) of the animals; but he is given curious genetic~like instructions on which animals to select and take.

The boat is longer than a football field, and, about the height of a modern "supertanker ship." In fact, modern engineers that have looked at the precise measurements given for the boat in the Book of Genesis have been stunned, calling it: "The most optimized for exactly the job it was built to do."

The animals also did NOT come in a neat line of pairs. Both Genesis & Jasher specify they came as giant herds that surrounded the boat, probably showing up for months.

As if something instinctively told them, a storm was coming... Are animals not generally a sign of such?

Noah was given special instructions on selecting the seven pairs of each clean animal; and the single pairs of each unclean animal.

107

Can the Boat Survive?

Building the Ark: Image Courtesy Answers in Genesis

With the Rage of the Waters, Things Freezing in Seconds in some Places.... Creatures hurled under Earth and Stone in Most Places....

It is Interesting Exactly Where the Boat Took off From.

The Boat Likely Didn't Go Far from where it Started.

It is Not really Designed to "Go Anywhere," just to Float and Survive.

Most of the Life on this Planet is Sea Life, then plants.

Both of these make the Planet after the Flood, as the Waters retire, a Rich Environment for Life to Flourish Rapidly Again.

Insects & Amphibians also covered the Continents via Floating Materials.

The Mammals (which only make a few Percentage Points of the Life on this Planet) were on the Boat.

If you Notice, the Place the Boat Left from (Beneath) is in the Dead Center of a MAssive Continent. Also, It is as Far from the Mid-Oceanic Ridge (Where the Water was Coming Out, highlighted in RED) as you could get.

Though the Boat probably Rose Fast, And was Terrifying.... It would have Survived.

Resting Atop the Waters... It would have then Softly Rocked the Animals inside to Deep Sleep.

THE BOAT OF NOAH
CAN ALL THE ANIMALS FIT?

If we go with the most absurdly high numbers we can muster then it would be 75,000 animals in total to get every creature today.

That would be 42% of the boat's capacity.

Noah's Ark has roughly the measurements of a modern day "SuperTanker ship."

In fact, its shipping capacity in modern terms would be roughly: 750 box cars.

NOAH'S ARK
750 RAIL CARS

NOAH'S ARK
17,550
× 2
―――――
35,000

→ 75,000
42%

If we go with more realistic numbers. The boat will hold 180,000. You would need only 21,000 of that.... Or, roughly 12% of the boat for the animal storage.

21,000
12%

The math for this is actually very simple. We are also in this example going to say all these animals are the size of a full size sheep (PS: most of the animals are nowhere near the size of a grown sheep).

80,000 ANIMALS

Yes... all the animals, and food for them, can fit... easily.

Blessings And Curses of the Three Sons

20 Now Noah, a man of the soil, proceeded to plant a vineyard. 21 But when he drank some of its wine, he became drunk and uncovered himself inside his tent. 22 And Ham, the father of Canaan, saw his father's nakedness and told his two brothers outside.

23 Then Shem and Japheth took a garment and placed it across their shoulders, and walking backward, they covered their father's nakedness. Their faces were turned away so that they did not see their father's nakedness.

24 When Noah awoke from his drunkenness and learned what his youngest son had done to him, 25 he said,

"Cursed be Canaan! A servant of servants shall he be to his brothers."

Coverings given to Adam & Eve

Adam → Noah

Coverings

Shem → Abraham

Noah → Japheth

Noah → Ham → Cush → Nimrod/EnMerkar

Ham → Canaan (Father of Canaanites)

26 He also declared: "Blessed be the LORD, the God of Shem! May Canaan be the servant of Shem.

27 May God expand the territory of Japheth; may he dwell in the tents of Shem,

and may Canaan be his servant!"

28 After the flood, Noah lived 350 years. 29 So Noah lived a total of 950 years, and then he died.

GENESIS 8:4
4 ON THE SEVENTEENTH DAY OF THE SEVENTH MONTH, THE ARK CAME TO REST ON THE MOUNTAINS OF ARARAT.

THIS IS THE SAME DAY JESUS CAME FROM THE TOMB, AND THE SAME DAY THE HEBREWS CROSSED THE RED SEA.

MT. ARARAT

IS 16 THOUSAND FEET TALL. THAT IS TALLER THAN THE TALLEST MOUNTAINS IN COLORADO. IT IS ON THE BORDER OF BOTH TURKEY AND ARMENIA.

THE MOUNTAIN RISES 11,000 FEET STRAIGHT UP.

THE TOP IS COVERED BY GLACIER ICE IN WHICH ANYTHING COULD BE FROZEN IN TIME.

THE WINDS AT THE TOP OF THE MOUNTAIN WOULD TERRIFY THE BEST HELICOPTER PILOT.

EXPLORERS DISCOVERED THAT LOCALS AT THE BASE OF THE MOUNTAIN ON THE ARMENIAN SIDE CALLED THE AREA:

"THE LAND OF THE EIGHT"

AS IF THAT WEREN'T ENOUGH, ALSO DISCOVERED THERE WERE THE REMAINS OF THE OLDEST WINE VINEYARDS ON EARTH.

OLDEST VINEYARDS

NOAH
A Trey Smith Project
Ancient Timeline

You have Six Ages of Empires beginning with the Tiny Sumerian/Assyrian settlements & Temples that begin to sprout up along the Tigris and Euphrates in Modern Day Iraq.

At the Death of Jesus, your Empires turn into religions.

Rome was never conquered. Its Bureaucracy became so Large it collapsed in on itself.... And today is called the Roman Catholic Church.

Therefore, some call this Time-Period "Rome-Phase II."

3300-2400BC

Pre-Flood → Flood → Nimrod ~ Sumerians → Assyrians → Egyptians → Babylonians → Persians → Greeks → Romans

Determining the date of the Flood is not as simple as it might seem. The exact date of the flood can change depending on the method of the mathematics used, the text used (Septuagint, Masoretic, or Samaritan), the calculations in Genesis 5 and 11 (and interpretation thereof), and the time each generation birthed children in those genealogies.

As strange as it may seem, the dates closer to 2400 BC can mathematically have a shockingly nice fit, particularly when we look at how "stretched" the modern Egyptian timelines are. And, as we learned earlier, population growth happens rapidly... Accordingly, in those days, families were breeding there own little armies of children.

But, a "tight fit" does not neccessarily mean a "Right Fit." We lay that in your hands. A general non-precise, rough date for the flood could be said to be in the ballpark of 3000 BC.

NOAH

Your first "Empires of Earth" begin in the same Area that the "boat that saved all mankind" landed, and also in EXACTLY the same time-frame.

They began their Empires in the Fertile Land (seen in Red) which comes down from Ararat Mountain (Turkey & Armenia) into Modern Iraq. Saudi Arabia, and Iran are on one Side. And, Egypt, Cush & ethiopia, into Africa on the other side.

This is called the Fertile Cresent, or Ancient Mesopotamia.

The FIRST three Major Empires To form were: Sumeria/Assyria, Egypt, then Babylon... In that Order.

Empires of the Ancient World were (at their Start) about the size of Modern shopping malls; with tiny mud brick homes fanning out for miles around them.

Sahara Desert is the Largest bald spot on Earth. It used to be the most fruitful jungle.

SAHARA
GARDEN OF EDEN?

LAND OF CUSH

Cush (or Kush) was the Oldest son of Noah's Son Ham. Cush had Four Sons... They would all become Nations and Peoples.

Those are:

Mizraim ~ Egypt
Phut ~ Libya
Canaan ~ Canaanites
Ham ~ Nimrod (Assyrians)

And Many others...

CRADLE OF CIVILIZATION
3300-2400 BC
SUMERIA/ASSYRIA
FIRST EMPIRES
LAND OF NIMROD

113

Ancient Mesopotamia
Where Life started again after the Flood

NOAH
MT. ARARAT

NINEVEH
City of Nimrud is next to Nineveh

BABYLONE
Later Babylon

KISH (CUSH)

URUK
Where Gilgamesh ruled
The First City in the World

UR
Where Abraham was born

Tigris & Euphrates Rivers

Ziggurat of Eridu
Tower of Babel

EGYPT

RED SEA

Ancient Population Growth

As you can see above, the First Cities of the Ancient World drop directly down from Mount Ararat; Where Lord Aratta (Noah) lived according to the Bible, Manetho the Historian of Egypt, and Enmerkar (Nimrod) in his Ancient writings.

World populations grow rapidly. For Example: If one family has 5 children, and those children have 5 children, and those 5, etc, etc, etc..... You come to 10 million people in roughly 10 generations (or the time Abraham was born). In the Ancient World, Five (5) children would be a very small family. By the Time Abraham was 40, it would have both likely & easily doubled to 20 million (at least).

114

ANSWERS IN GENESIS
ARK ReCreation

Noah's Ark was not just a literal event in the history of our world. it is also a symbolism from God to man.

"Enter through the narrow gate. For wide is the gate and broad is the road that leads to destruction, and many enter through it. But small is the gate and narrow the road that leads to life, and only a few find it."

Matthew 7:13-14

Noah's Ark

Like the Two Trees in the garden, or Two Paths, the occult has favored the Raven, the Falcon, the Crow...

Whilst God favors the Dove.

The dove who returned with an Olive Branch ~ the Symbol for Israel ~ in its mouth to Noah on the Boat.

The Dove is a Symbol of Hope, the Spirit of God, Peace and Freedom.

The Raven is a Symbol of Darkness and Bondage.

The Raven

Eye of Horus

Horus
Part Man/Part God, birthed from Dead God Osiris & Isis. Symbol of the Falcon from the Boat.

Garuda
Bird of Lord Vishnu. Lord Vishnu is King of Air where he Rules from his bed of Naga Serpents.

The Dove

Luke 3:22

When all the people were being baptized, Jesus was baptized too. And as He was praying, heaven was opened, and the Holy Spirit descended on Him in a bodily form like a dove. And a voice came from heaven: "You are My beloved Son; in You I am well pleased." Jesus Himself was about thirty years old when He began His ministry.

Genesis 3

21 The Lord God made garments of skin for Adam and his wife and clothed them.

Adam → Noah Coverings

Jasher 3

14 And it was in the fifty-sixth year of the life of Lamech when Adam died; nine hundred and thirty years old was he at his death, and his two sons, with Enoch and Methuselah his son, buried him with great pomp, as at the burial of kings, in the cave which God had told him.

**Methuselah died at 969, the oldest living man.

His name means: "His Death Shall Bring" (The Judgment). He died seven days before the flood.

No-one lived over 1000 yrs ~ or one day to God. "In the day you eat of the tree, you shall die."

Methuselah - the oldest living tree in the world in Bristlecone Pine Forest 4849 years old

This was the first sacrifice. Something innocent would have to die for the covering of sins.

Jesus would be the Adam that did not fail, the last sacrifice covering sins.

Jesus came through the bloodline of Shem.

שׁ Shin 300

Shem is the hidden name for God.

116

Some say it would be impossible for anyone from the Ancient World to build the ship described in Genesis....

Is That a Joke?

The Ancient World is full of Giant Building Projects That Baffle and Amaze us....

Noah → Shem → Abraham
Noah → Japheth
Noah → Ham → Cush → Nimrod/EnMerkar

One Would Literally Expect to Find Giant Building Projects Coming Right Through the Bloodlines of a Family Such as This....

And Speaking of Giant Building Projects, That Brings us to Nimrod and his Tower.

NIMROD

117

THE END
Part One

The Journey Continues in
NIMROD
God in a Nutshell proJect

www.ingramcontent.com/pod-product-compliance
Lightning Source LLC
Chambersburg PA
CBHW041952150426

43198CB00004B/106